"I don't care if I don't have s...
I'm never going to take it from someone." – Danny

To the Survivors

One Man's Journey as a Rape Crisis Counselor with
True Stories of Sexual Violence

Robert Uttaro

Robert Uttaro does not give medical advice or prescribe the use of any technique as a form of treatment for physical, emotional, or medical problems without the advice of a physician, either directly or indirectly. This book is not a substitute for legal, medical, psychological, or other health care professional advice and treatment. Robert Uttaro cares about helping people impacted by sexual violence, but he recommends you see qualified lawyers, legal advocates, physicians, therapists, psychologists, psychiatrists and other health care professionals regarding your legal and individual health needs.

This book is dedicated to all who have been affected by sexual violence.

Some of the names and places in this book have been changed to protect confidentiality. Also, I will not use the real name of the organization I worked for as a volunteer. To protect confidentiality, I will refer to that organization as "The Healing Place" and "THP".

A portion of proceeds from the sale of this book will be donated to rape crisis centers.

CONTENTS

———

March Fourteenth

Here is a list, God, of everything I'm never forgetting.

Burns on her legs.
Impressions of his hands around her neck.
The all over purple-ly skin.
She can not
will not
can not
will not
can not
will not do the internal part of that effing kit, no.

(I hang back in the waiting room as they implore her for hours and pray they will...oh-my-god...stop raping.)

She can not
will not
can not
will not
can not
will not
can not
will not say his name, no.

(She gives up, writes alphabet letters only kind of true; no matter love, I understand you.)

A 72-hour psych hold.
Cops and detectives.
My brother-in-law in rare tears the morning not-one-of-us-slept after.
Silence all these years.
And the prize for speaking? A brand new horror show.
Doesn't seem worth it now or ever.
She never feels clean.

She'll never.
Not after a hundred hospital showers.

Her fear of the past.
Her fear of today.
Her fear of tomorrow and every hour before and after this moment.
Overwhelming.
The questions.
The shaking.
The stares of strangers and remembering when.
(I'm struggling not to vomit. We're trying not to live this.)

"Can they see it on me?" She wonders like before.
"Why can't they see it, the secret I can't say?"

She says prayers, but not like the ones she prays when he comes home to
decide, "I miss your mother" and "You know, you're so pretty."

Try again. I see a light in the sky.

Your heart is broken.
My heart is broken.
Our heart is bro-ken.

(But... try them again.)

-A poem Jenee wrote in response to visiting her friend in the hospital who
was beaten, choked, burned, and raped.

INTRODUCTION

———

"This book is not about statistics."

I never thought I would volunteer at a rape crisis center. I always knew rape and sexual assault existed, but for most of my life I did not seriously consider ways in which I could help those affected by sexual violence. I could not imagine that a large number of people actually experience such an evil and detrimental horror as rape is, but unfortunately many do. Never in my wildest dreams did I think I would help play a positive role in the healing process of rape and sexual assault survivors, educate people, and be active in the fight against sexual violence, but often times our lives go in different directions than we plan or expect.

Sexual violence is very complex. Given that, I will not speak for every human being who has been affected by this crime. This book is by no means a blue print of how all rapes and sexual assaults occur, nor will I tell you how to feel. I do not have all of the answers to the many difficult questions that arise when discussing sexual violence, and I obviously do not know everyone who has experienced sexual violence. This book is about my experiences as a rape crisis counselor and the survivors I have met who felt strong enough and comfortable enough to share their stories with me and you. I have my opinions and ideas about different aspects of sexual violence, but neither I nor the people you will soon meet speak for humanity. Everyone's story is his or her own. Everyone's story is different. Growth and healing is different for everyone.

Sexual violence is not only a violent crime, but it is also a serious health issue. It affects people's bodies, minds, hearts, and souls. I do not wish to name anyone's experiences or claim knowledge of all the effects people may feel as a result of sexual violence, but I do know some things. I have learned that many survivors of sexual violence feel shame. Shame directly causes a variety of negative health issues, including mentalities about one's self and behaviors. I hope to attempt to alleviate some of that shame through this book.

I have always cared about people and the world we all live in. As long as I can remember, I have been intrigued by the complexities of the human experience and questioned what it means to be human. It is fascinating to me that some people are happy, fulfilled, or loving, while others are unhappy, unfulfilled, or hateful. Even as a young boy, I questioned, *Why is there so much hatred and violence in the world? Why do some people hate other people? Why do some people hurt other people? Why do some people rape other people? Why do some people kill other people?* I have come to understand that I may never know the answers to these questions and many of the other difficult life questions that people contemplate, but one thing I do know is this: There are far too many men, women, and children who are sexually violated. It is my opinion that we are foolish if we do not take the issue of sexual violence seriously and help play a positive role in the healing process of individuals who experience it, as well as those indirectly impacted by it.

Throughout my life, I have been very empathetic toward the suffering of others. I contemplated the effects of violence, but I never did enough about the problems that I saw because I felt insecure. I didn't think my voice mattered. I could easily discuss the variety of life issues with family and friends in my own home, but I did not have the confidence within myself to step out of my comfort zone. I had the passion deep down inside of me to help in some kind of way, but my insecure illusions about myself and my abilities crippled me. Given my insecurities, I never once thought I would join an organization whose purpose was to help any person affected by sexual violence at no cost to him or her, but I'm glad I broke down my own ridiculous barriers. Ultimately, making the choice to volunteer at The Healing Place changed my life and allowed me to impact the lives of some.

Volunteering at THP has been the most fulfilling aspect of my life. The work has allowed me to teach and help people on their healing journeys. I have even managed to inspire some people to get active and volunteer. One of the most meaningful things I have done in my life is plant a seed in people's minds about THP's existence. I look at it like this: How can people get the help and services they need if they don't even know those services exist in or near their community?

Some people think that volunteering at a rape crisis center is morbid and depressing. For me, that has been true at times given the severity and intensity of the work. However, in my experiences, the good has far outweighed the bad. I have met some of the sweetest, most compassionate, caring, talented, and strong individuals while doing this work. The people I have worked alongside and the survivors with whom I have interacted inspire me in a variety of ways. They have helped me to become a better listener, counselor, and public speaker. Because of their example, I have learned a tremendous amount about these issues and gained more confidence in myself. I am blessed to have been accepted by THP and become a part of their family.

My experiences as a counselor have been painful and fulfilling. My heart has been broken and uplifted many times, but my spirit and faith have never left me. I've seen a lot of pain and heard a lot of horrible stories. I have listened to some of the most disturbing things possible. Sometimes what seems like a lie and impossible is the truth and possible. Some people experience vile crimes and live with painful memories that others cannot believe could even happen. Yet in such adversity, the strength of rape survivors is incredibly inspirational.

It is at times incomprehensible to acknowledge that such disturbing crimes are committed against others and then meditate on the damaging effects of those crimes. My journey as a rape crisis counselor and the stories you will read in this book are less than a fraction of the whole picture of survivors, perpetration, and sexual violence. But at least this is something. I hope this book can give anyone who reads it some sense of clarity, strength, and hope, as well as another opportunity for growing and healing if needed.

This book is not about statistics. The statistics are certainly out there; you can research and read them for yourself if you want to. I, however, will not share or focus on statistics because I do not want to treat people as numbers. Also, I believe rape and sexual assault are the least reported violent crimes. If it is true that these are the least reported crimes, then that means most of the people who experience these crimes are not represented in those statistics. To me, giving flawed and inaccurate statistics of rape and sexual assault is a disservice to those who do not report.

I believe there are many justified reasons why most people do not report, but I will mention two major reasons: First, many survivors do not report because they fear they will not be believed. Many have an image in their head about what a victim should look like because of the media and therefore will not report. Second, it is extremely difficult to report a violent crime against someone that is known to the person. Most survivors know their perpetrators, and the relationship between them makes reporting even harder than it might have been if the crime were perpetrated by a stranger. The bottom line is none of us will be able to understand the full extent of how common sexual violence is based on statistics because the statistics are only a fraction of what really occurs.

My simple truth when discussing the prevalence of sexual violence is this: I don't know. I simply do not know how many people have been raped or sexually assaulted, nor do I know how many instances of violation have occurred in a single person's life. I also do not know how many people have been indirectly impacted by sexual violence or how many cases of indirect impact have occurred in a single person's life. No one knows.

I have to warn you before you continue reading that this book is graphic at times and may be triggering if you are a survivor. You will read people's own words about their rape or multiple experiences with sexual violence. You will also have a chance to hear how the crime has affected them, how they have dealt with it, and how they have grown in their healing process. This book will be hard to read at times, and again, I have to stress that it may be triggering for some. With that, however, I encourage you that this book reflects and offers immense strength and hope.

In this book you will read the real stories of real people. I believe these stories will incite emotions and possibly painful memories. I highly suggest you read this book with a loved one near you, either in person or on the phone. This of course can be a family member, friend, therapist, religious or spiritual guide, or anyone else. Stay close to someone you love and trust. However, I also completely understand if you want to read this alone and not share with anyone. I just want to provide you with all possible options of ways to read these pages moving forward. Please take care of yourself, and do whatever it is that makes you feel better before, during, and after reading this book.

You do not have to read this book if it is too personal or too hard. There are resources and trained professionals that can help you or anyone you know. If you find you need help or information, I implore you to search for rape crisis centers in your area on the internet. For example, through a simple online query, I located sixteen rape crisis centers in Wyoming in only ten seconds. If you can't read the whole book or even parts of it, please try to find a rape crisis center in your area and make that phone call. I want this book to be helpful, not hurtful.

I believe it is imperative to mention that you will read the word "survivor" throughout this book. I use this term because that is the term I was trained to use when referring to people who have been raped or sexually assaulted. Many people embrace this term and identify with it. However, not everyone identifies with this term. In fact, some people hate the term "survivor", including those who have been raped and sexually assaulted.

This word does not reflect how everyone chooses to identify themselves, but I will use it for the purposes of this book.

This book is dedicated to all who have been affected by sexual violence. I have learned throughout this journey that anyone can be raped or sexually assaulted, regardless of gender, age, ethnicity, religion, socio-economic status or sexual orientation. This is true from infants to the elderly. Sexual violence is very detrimental, and I hope to alleviate some of that detriment. I hope that anyone who has been affected by sexual violence will seek out help if they need it. I hope people will become more educated on the realities and prevalence of sexual violence. I hope to challenge rape myths and have people think about this crime differently than they may currently think about it. I hope people stop blaming survivors for being raped and start believing and listening to them. I hope this book helps empower those who feel lost and disempowered. I simply hope this book somehow helps, however you may define help for yourself if you need it.

Chapter 1

CHILDHOOD

———

"I cut myself when I was a little kid. I do not label myself a cutter, but I have cut. I took a kitchen knife and brought it into the bathtub with me, where I proceeded to cut my whole left forearm. I did not cut deep enough to leave scars, but my whole forearm, from my elbow to my wrist, was covered in red cuts. I told my friend Aaliyah that I fell in thorns. She believed me."

People often ask me, "Why did you join The Healing Place?" A lot of people think that I was raped, which I guess is a decent assumption given that I volunteered at a rape crisis center. I wasn't raped. At least not that I know of. Later in this book you will meet Don, a man who was raped by his uncle at the tender age of four. He didn't even know he had been sexually abused until over fifty years later. Sexual violence is very traumatic and memory loss is real. So is it possible that I experienced sexual abuse as a child? Yes. Do I have any memory of it? No. So as of the writing of this book, I would say the following to those people: No, I have not been raped or sexually assaulted.

I was born on April 4, 1985. Two months prior to my birth, Cardinal Bernard Law of the Boston Archdiocese visited my parents' local church. My mother, being the devout Catholic woman she is, went to her church with genuine excitement to meet Cardinal Law. She hoped to receive a blessing for her fifth and final child from the Cardinal. My mother waited at the end of a long line in the back of the church for this special moment. When she finally met Cardinal Law, he could obviously see my mother was seven months pregnant. Cardinal Law touched my mother's stomach and said to her, "I'm going to bless you for a healthy baby and for you a quick, easy delivery."

The water came out meconium-stained when the doctor broke my mother's water. My mother feared that I was dead. The doctor said, "I think the cord is around the baby's neck." When they delivered and my head came out, the doctor unraveled the cord from around my neck three times. I swallowed a lot of meconium, so they alerted the pediatrician immediately. As soon as I was born, attendants rushed me to a table so that the pediatrician could suck the meconium out of my throat with a tube. Thankfully, the meconium did not enter my lungs and I did not die. Afterwards, the obstetrician said, "By the color of the placenta, I think the cord was wrapped around the neck for two months." My mother thinks it is ironic that the umbilical cord began to wrap around my neck at the same time Cardinal Law touched her stomach and "blessed her". I think it's more than ironic.

I was born on Holy Thursday. Holy Thursday is a day celebrated by Catholics and other Christian denominations to commemorate the Last Supper. In the Bible, the Last Supper is the story of when Jesus ate dinner and drank wine with his friends, better known as his disciples, before being arrested, imprisoned, beaten mercilessly, humiliated, and crucified. My parents left the hospital after three days on Easter Sunday, which is celebrated by Catholics and Christians as the Resurrection of Jesus Christ, and brought me to Sunday mass. I was in a Catholic Church before I was in a home.

I grew up the youngest of five in an Italian/Irish/Scottish American Catholic household. Religion was always a big part of my life mainly because of my family and the fact that I had to go to a Catholic school for seven years. When I was in the first grade, my parents attended a teacher conference where my teacher at the time told them, "The old nuns would point to Robert and say he has a vocation." Some may think that statement means I should have become a Catholic priest. Who knew the old nuns were actually right, except my vocation was not to be a Catholic priest; it was to try my best to help rape survivors.

In August of 2007, I completed my training to be a rape crisis counselor with the sole purpose of helping rape survivors in any way possible. I didn't care if I organized files, swept the floors, or cleaned the toilets – I just wanted to help. I never thought of the possibility that I was sexually abused because I never had memories of being sexually abused, but I learned over time that some people thought I had been. The seed became planted in my head when a full-time rape crisis counselor disclosed to me that an older relative had sexually abused her. After she disclosed, she looked at me like it was my turn. It seemed like she wanted me to disclose, even though I never once thought I was sexually abused myself. I say that based on her eyes, facial expressions, and the inquiring silence that hung between us after she spoke. I had never experienced an interaction like this before – an interaction that is impossible to truly describe through words.

To not have memories of being sexually abused, and then have a certified counselor instill the possibility of me being sexually abused was disturbing and frightening. A certified counselor planted the worst possible seed in my mind, which to me is blatantly unprofessional and morally abhorrent. Because of this counselor, for the first time in my life I asked myself the question: *Did it happen to me?* That night really fucked me up in my mind and I started to go crazy.

I began to spend a lot of time in deep thought contemplating my past, but specifically my childhood. I cut myself when I was a little kid. I do not label myself a cutter, but I have cut. I took a kitchen knife and brought it into the bathtub with me, where I proceeded to cut my whole left forearm. I did not cut deep enough to leave scars, but my whole forearm, from my elbow to my wrist, was covered in red cuts. I told my friend Aaliyah that I fell in thorns. She believed me.

During this time of adult reminiscence, I called Aaliyah.

"Aaliyah, do you remember when I fell in thorns?"

She did.

I asked, "How old was I?"

"Bobby, you were in the fourth grade."

On a different night I asked, "Aaliyah, do you remember when I became an altar boy?"

"The fourth grade."

I broke down and cried that night, which historically was very hard for me to do.

Memories started to come. I hated the Catholic school that I went to as a little kid. After the first day of first grade, I said to my mother, "Ma, I'm ready to go back to my old school." I had to attend this school for seven years until my parents listened to my pleas and finally let me leave. I didn't even care about graduating with my best friends; I just wanted out. The school that I went to taught me valuable life lessons on hypocrisy. For the purposes of this book, I will only write about the allegations of priests breaking their vows of celibacy, sexual abuse, and an arrest of one priest.

Priests and nuns lived next to the school, which became known to some of us as a transition school. The priests used to get transferred in and out, to and from different parishes. For some reason the nuns never did. When I was in the second grade, the most popular priest was transferred. The people loved him and expressed sadness at seeing him leave. Some people questioned why he left. Much of the information that circulated on his departure suggested he had been sent to help poor people in the ghettos. Many people seemed upset because they believed they had lost the coolest, funniest, and most charismatic priest: Father Jackson. Father Jackson was rumored to have had sex with a lot of women even though he had taken a vow of celibacy.

I do not have proof of Father Jackson or any of the other priests at my school breaking their vows of celibacy or sexually abusing children. I will however mention one rumor of Father Thompson and one arrest of Father Tim. At the time, Father Thompson held the position of head priest, which meant he controlled the parish. He drove a Mercedes and reeked of alcohol every day. A rumor persisted that he had had a "relationship" with a young boy. I do not believe that an arrest ever occurred, nor do I know if the allegations were true. Father Tim, however, was arrested.

As adults, my friend Tito said to me one day, "Dude, did you hear about Father Tim?"

"Who the hell is Father Tim," I said.

"Are you serious? He was a priest at our school. He got arrested for following a guy into the woods and sexually assaulting him."

"Get the hell outta here."

"Dude, check it out."

Tito pulled up the news article on my computer. Father Tim had been arrested for indecent assault and battery, but the charges were eventually dropped. I started to remember Father Tim once I saw his face from the article. My initial reaction was rage. I wanted to stab Tim in his throat with the sharpest knife I could find. My own reaction scared me. I'm not saying I'm proud of my anger or right in how I reacted, but this is how I felt in the moment.

It is important to note that there are some truly amazing Catholic priests throughout the world, but I do not believe they existed at my school or the church where I served as an altar boy. I believe that some of the priests repeatedly moved in and out were guilty of sexual abuse, but my beliefs ultimately don't matter. I have no proof or evidence, so I cannot say anything with any certainty. But just because someone is not found guilty in a court of law does not mean a crime or multiple crimes have not occurred or will not occur in the future.

Sexual abuse exists in every religion, but the sexual abuse scandal within the Catholic Church that became known to the public started in Massachusetts. Catholic priests accused of sexual abuse were moved from parish to parish to parish under the supervision of Cardinal Law. Instead of punishment, the Catholic Church chose to welcome Cardinal Law into Vatican City. Cardinal Bernard Law, the man who "blessed" my mother for a healthy birth of me, was never incarcerated for his role in allowing little boys to be raped and sexually assaulted.

The sexual abuse scandal within the Catholic Church has always affected me. If I'm honest with myself, I have to acknowledge that I served as an altar boy before the scandal came to fruition. This makes me question the possibility of being sexually abused given that some (not all) altar boys were raped and I started cutting myself at or around the same time I became an altar boy. However, I am of the firm belief that I was not sexually abused given that I have no memories of ever being sexually abused.

The more I contemplated on my past, the more memories came. Sadly, the same certified rape crisis counselor who made me think I was sexually abused, along with others, has questioned my motives for volunteering at a rape crisis center. For some reason, these insecure and confused individuals didn't have the decency to attempt to think of how I have been affected by sexual violence without being raped or sexually assaulted.

Throughout my life I have seen sexual violence in movies, TV shows, on the news, in music, and in music videos. I have been listening to music that deals with issues of sexual violence since my childhood. Listening to intense music, screams, or reading emotional lyrics has always affected me. I remember listening to a song about child rape, and I immediately said to my friend, "Do you hear this? Do you fuckin hear this?" I have always been affected by sexual violence and I always cared. Even since a young age, I questioned what it all meant.

Not only have I seen sexual violence in music and in the media throughout my life, but I have known rape and sexual assault survivors as well. One of my good friends was molested by one of her family members. She and

I have never spoken of it, but I always cared. In the only way I knew how to speak about such vileness, I wrote a heavy metal song for her and for anyone else like her when I was in high school. The song was solely about rape. I excitedly gave my lyrics to my other guitarist hoping that he would like what I had written. I actually believed he would be just as excited to create a brutal heavy metal song and speak out against such sickness. Unfortunately, he laughed at me and thought I was crazy. He didn't get it. We did not create music to the lyrics and I never tried to write lyrics again. I felt alone in my thinking and continued to feel sad for my friend who had been abused.

It saddens me to acknowledge that those individuals who have questioned my motives for volunteering at a rape crisis center did not attempt to understand me, my loved ones, the people I spoke to, and the people I will never meet. They only seemed to think that I had been sexually abused and questioned my motives for reasons I do not understand. They somehow did not even seem to consider my care for others. That kind of thinking is simply ignorant and ridiculous, and they are wrong. However, their beliefs about my potential sexual abuse confused me and made me go crazy for at least two years.

Chapter 2

GETTING INVOLVED

——

"I did not call for this work, but rather, I was called to it."

Whether I was sexually abused or not is ultimately irrelevant. The truth is you don't have to personally experience something to care about something. I care about gang violence, but I've never been in a gang, nor do I want to join one. I care about prison reform, but I've never been incarcerated. I care that children die of starvation, but I've been blessed that my parents were able to put food on the table for my four siblings and I. I think and care about many things, such as the existence or non-existence of God. I often contemplate what it means if God exists, as well as what it means if God does not exist. I personally believe "good" exists, and I believe "evil" exists. I think about evil, because I see a lot of evil in the world. To me, rape is one of the most evil crimes in existence, and I felt a calling to combat that evil in some way.

In my last semester at college, my professor assigned a book that taught me a lot about rape and the aftermath of what can happen to survivors. Thankfully, I became more educated on the reality that is sexual violence. My commentary on these learning experiences is short and simple: I've always known people hurt people. I've always known rape exists. I've always believed evil exists. What I didn't know, and learned over time, is that many rape survivors are treated horrendously by others. What I didn't know is how much victim blaming occurs to survivors. The victim blaming that I began to learn about drove me insane. I felt disgusted, horrified, and sad, yet this ignited a passion deep within to do something about it.

During class, our professor told us that staff from THP would come and speak to us. He also said there would be volunteer opportunities for anyone who wanted to volunteer. I didn't know if I would volunteer or not, but I knew I had to attend that class because I really wanted to listen to people who chose to do this kind of work full-time.

After a few minutes of lecture from my professor, Carmen and Aila walked into the classroom. Carmen led the Community Outreach Department and Aila led the Legal Department. They both spoke so gently, yet I heard strength in their voices. They looked and sounded like some of the sweetest people in the world. I sat in my chair and listened to them speak about sexual violence and THP. I watched them in awe and admiration of the fact that they dedicated a part of their lives to educating the public and helping anyone affected by sexual violence.

For the first time in my life, I heard about "The Healing Place". THP offers free and confidential services to survivors of rape and sexual assault, as well as their family members and friends. THP's services include a 24-hour hotline, 24-hour emergency room accompaniment, counseling, legal assistance, case management services, and educational workshops. I thought this place was amazing. I truly admired THP's existence and presence in communities.

I thought to myself, *I'm twenty-two, and I just heard about this place now. Why? Why doesn't everyone know about this place?* I then thought to myself, *How the hell do Carmen, Aila, and everyone else at THP do this kind of work on a full time basis?* I then contemplated how strong these women must have been. To say I was impressed by this place is an understatement. I felt deep respect, gratitude, and some sense of kinship with all who made the choice to join and actively participate at THP.

Carmen told the students she was going to have us watch a DVD. She warned us that the DVD contained disturbing material and that we could leave the room if we wanted to. Carmen explained to us that the DVD was a re-enactment of an interview with a rapist. I sat back in my chair not having a clue as to what I was about to watch.

The rapist in the DVD was in a college fraternity. He and his frat brothers would scope out women throughout the week and then invite them to one of their parties. While at the party, he and his frat scumbags would purposely get the women drunk. Once they were hammered, he and his frat criminals would rape them. Their attacks were premeditated, conscious, and violent.

It is important to note that this DVD does not speak for every fraternity member, nor does it explain how all forms of sexual perpetration occur. This was just one DVD of one criminal in one fraternity, but it was enough to drive me crazy.

My rage came out while I was watched in horror. I became a lunatic. I wanted to lunge through the TV screen and choke this pathetic excuse for a human being. I literally wanted to squeeze his throat until he couldn't breathe, worse than what he had done to his victim when he held her down and raped her. I wanted to stomp his head on cement over and over. Again, I'm not proud of my anger, but it's how I initially reacted. My rage then turned to disgust. I felt nauseous and thought I was going to throw up on the floor. I thought, *How could anyone do this?*

I cringed in my chair throughout the whole DVD. I couldn't believe I was watching this scumbag easily talk about a rape he had committed as if he were causally discussing cooking cod fish in a white wine sauce with roasted potatoes and asparagus. I couldn't believe some people commit this kind of crime and think nothing of it. All I could think of after my rage and nausea was, *This is so fucked up. This is not okay. This is too fucked up. I have to do something about this. I have to somehow do something.*

Carmen and Aila answered our questions and then continued on with their training. They explained to us that rape is really more about power and control and not about sex. I had never heard anyone say that before. I thought about what that meant.

They also explained that many survivors aren't even believed when they are strong enough to disclose their rape to someone. Sometimes even family members don't believe survivors. That horrified me. I got the sense that survivors are more apt to heal when they are believed, listened to, supported, and not blamed. In my mind I found myself screaming, *Are ya fuckin kiddin me! They aren't believed?! Why wouldn't you believe someone?! How sick is that! People blame rape survivors?! For what?! For being raped?! How can you actually do that?!* I was psychotic in my mind and probably looked like a maniac in my seat.

Carmen and Aila said THP promotes healing. These two women taught me that just listening to a survivor truly helps them in their healing process. I thought to myself, *I would believe someone. I would just listen. I know in my heart that I will give unconditional support to people affected by sexual violence.* Based on what Carmen and Aila said, I thought I could somehow help by the simplest means of listening, not judging, and not blaming.

Toward the end of class, Carmen and Aila described various volunteer opportunities to us. I sensed a calling to volunteer, but I can't fully explain how nervous I felt. I knew I wanted to ask, but I was terrified. My own insecurities immediately came into play. An overwhelming list of negatives filled my mind. These negatives included:

1. I'm a man. They might not even accept men.
2. I won't be good at counseling.
3. I'll make someone feel worse.
4. I'll somehow hurt as opposed to help.
5. My voice doesn't even matter.
6. I can't do it.
7. I suck. What the hell makes me think I can actually help rape survivors?

I was hard on myself, but that's how I thought at the time. I could only think about how bad I would be as opposed to thinking, *I actually can help rape survivors.* As nervous and sweaty as I was, I said, "fuck it".

Shaking, I walked up to Aila and asked, "Can I volunteer?" She said, "Of course! We'd love the help, but there is an interview process. Write down your contact information and someone will get back to you." Saying the words "fuck it" and just doing it turned out to be the best decision I could have ever made.

THP contacted me a few weeks later for an interview with Aila and Joan, the Case Manager. As soon as I saw their faces and looked in their eyes I felt at peace. Their kindness erased all of my very intense anxieties. I knew instantly that I had made the right choice.

Aila and Joan talked about THP and the case management internship for which I intended to apply. After they explained more about their work and what the position entailed, they asked me why I wanted to volunteer at THP. I spoke from the heart. I told them that I think it is wrong to blame people who are raped. I told them that I will always believe people, listen to them, and never blame them no matter what. I told them that I wanted to just help. I simply stressed I wanted to help in any way, shape, or form. That was it. That was all I cared about.

A few weeks later I got the call. I became ecstatic once I learned that I ended up beating a few people out for the case manager internship. I couldn't even believe it. It shocked me that I had been picked over other women and that THP would choose me over other people. I was excited, but terrified. I thought to myself, *I can't believe I'm actually doing this.* Turns out I joined only a handful of men to ever work at THP, which I think is sad.

I never once thought I would be a rape crisis counselor. I did not go to school with the ambition of getting involved at a rape crisis center, but the class I took in college began a life change for me, and my vocation started unraveling from there. I did not call for this work, but rather, I was called to it. That may be hard to understand, but I will try my best to explain it.

This book is not about religion. I am not preaching God to you. People can and do believe what they want to believe. Billions of people believe in some kind of Higher Being. We all have the choice to believe in something greater than ourselves or not believe in something greater than ourselves. I personally believe God exists, and I believe God communicates with all of us through different means every day. This can be through music, art, nature, people, suffering, and other means. I believe that God spoke directly to me once I started reading the book that was assigned for class, and especially on that night when THP made their presentation to us. I believe God asked me to join THP in that moment, so I listened and chose to act on that request. I'm very thankful that I did and that THP gave me an opportunity. The six years following that decision have been extremely emotional, difficult, fun, educational, and more fulfilling than anything I could have ever imagined in my whole life. I've truly been blessed, and I try my best to share those blessings with others.

Chapter 3

MARY

———

"Can I be your first client?"

Before you can volunteer at THP you have to first complete an intense training. I didn't know what the training would entail, how many people would be there, or how I would even handle listening about rape for forty hours. I was excited about what the future held for me even though I felt nervous and terrified. This would be the first time I had ever done something like this in my life, and the seriousness and sensitivity of sexual violence only increased my fears.

I went to a party the night before the first day of training. I drank all night and somehow came across a woman named Mary. Mary spoke about her career goals of helping people, so I naturally, and probably rudely, interrupted her to join the conversation. It turns out Mary wanted to help children for her career. We ended up having a very interesting conversation about her goals, societal problems, and humanity.

I told her that I too wanted to help people, and that I was really interested in the criminal justice system and prison. I then said, "I'm actually going to work at a rape crisis center. I start my training tomorrow." Her whole demeanor changed.

She said, "Are you serious?"

"Yeah," I nodded. "I'm nervous as hell."

She said, "Can I be your first client?"

I blanked. "Huh? What do you mean?"

I didn't get it at first. I didn't understand what had happened, but then I did. Mary then disclosed to me that she was raped in college.

Mary and I kept in touch over the years. I called Mary one day to tell her about my progress on the book and asked her if she wanted to share her story. She was so excited! I asked if she wanted to speak or write. She said she would rather write, but she didn't know what to write about. I told her she could write about anything she wanted to. During our conversation, Mary told me that she was in the best place in her life. She described being happy and fulfilled. I couldn't have been happier for her. I told her she should write about the fullness of joy in her life. She agreed and seemed to be looking forward to it.

I did not hear back from Mary for awhile. I sent her text messages and emails, but she did not respond. I didn't want to push her, but I really thought her story should be in this book. I felt a little confused as to why she didn't respond back. I wasn't sure if she had forgotten about writing, or become uninterested in writing. I was wrong on both. Mary texted me and told me she had decided not to contribute. She said that she was in a really good place and was hesitant to re-open up.

Mary, I support your decision and am happy that you are in such a good place. I wish you all the best. Keep doing all that you do for yourself and for the children you help in your job. Love and peace girl. Be well.

-Bobby

Chapter 4

TRAINING

————

"I knew sexual violence affected people, but I did not know to what extent. I didn't fully understand that there really is a larger health issue at play."

I felt sick to my stomach before my intense training as I nervously walked into the training room. I sat in the back of the room and glanced around. No men. My anxiety grew worse by the seconds. More and more women kept walking into the room. No men. We started the training at 9am. Still no men. Me and about thirty women ranging from ages eighteen to sixty-five were about to spend forty hours over the course of a week together. I sat there shaking and sweating profusely, but I soon learned I had nothing to worry about.

The women in that room were some of the kindest and gentlest people I have ever met. I felt comfortable and accepted within ten minutes of being present. It is hard to explain this, but I felt a sense of camaraderie even though I had never met these people before. I even felt a sense of peace with these strangers. It was special to be a part of something larger than ourselves, and I found it inspirational to be with so many people who cared about the same issue and wanted to actually do something about it. I used to talk a lot. It was nice to finally do something.

The training was educational, intense, emotional, depressing, comical and enjoyable. The counselors amazed me. I remember listening to them give their presentations and looking at them with the utmost admiration. I was in awe of everyone and fascinated to meet other counselors who worked at a rape crisis center full-time. I wanted to learn so much from them because I valued their expertise and experiences.

The first day consisted of ground rules, expectations, ice breaker exercises, confidentiality, rape trauma, and empowerment. I learned on this day that some survivors actually expect to die during an assault. I also learned that some people dissociate during an assault, and most, if not all, have the goal to survive. The immediate impact after an assault can cause self-blame, shame, confusion, denial, persistent re-experiencing of the assault, and memory loss. This is not true for every person, but these are some common impacts post-assault.

I also learned of all of the potential effects a survivor may feel, either post-assault or even years later. This is not true for everyone, but here are some potential effects that result from sexual violence:

- Shame.
- Guilt.
- Depression.
- Sadness.
- Loss of Control.
- Vulnerability.
- Fear.
- Anger.
- Anxiety.
- Shock.
- Disbelief.
- Embarrassment.

- Becoming suicidal or committing suicide.
- Isolation.
- Distrust.
- Self medication or self harm in a variety of different ways such as substance abuse, cutting or burning.
- Changes in eating patterns.
- Changes in sleeping.
- Startle responses.
- Nightmares.
- Confusion.
- Difficulty concentrating.
- Safety concerns.

I knew sexual violence affected people, but I did not know to what extent. I didn't fully understand that there really is a larger health issue at play. At the end of the day, we had a check-out question where the presenters asked what we were going to do for self-care when we went home. I found it interesting to listen to so many different people explain the different things that put them at peace. I needed to learn some for myself. I was thankful we did such a great exercise because the first day was emotionally and mentally draining. THP stresses the importance of "self-care". I started to understand what they meant because I needed some.

The second day started with a check-in question, followed by a presentation on how to support male rape survivors. The presenter asked us, "Where does male rape occur?" We gave answers such as "Prison, in some churches (abuse scandal), and in homes." It was eye opening to learn about male survivors because I did not often hear people speak about the issue. I have often heard joking statements like, "Don't drop the soap in the shower", referring to men incarcerated. The truth, however, is it is completely irrelevant whether an inmate can hold the soap or not. A male inmate will find a way to rape another male inmate if he wants to. Prison rape is very real. Some inmates are gang raped. Some inmates become property of other inmates and are bought and sold. It's not funny; it's actually quite disturbing and more common than we know. The United States of America currently has the highest incarceration rate in the world, which has led to overcrowded prisons. Prison rape for both men and women is a severe problem that should be taken seriously.

After our training on male rape, we spent three hours learning about counseling and coping skills. We learned that coping skills can be positive and negative, helpful and destructive. For example, healthy coping skills can develop into strengths, such as doing well in school, in sports, at work, or being self-sufficient in a variety of different ways. Unhealthy coping skills, such as substance abuse or self-mutilation can be self-defeating and fatal. We learned that many survivors are hard on themselves and feel ashamed towards the way they coped during or after the crisis of rape. However, any coping strategy, either healthy or unhealthy, is not to be ashamed of. People most often do what they have to do in order to survive.

The third day started with another check-in question. We then participated in a training on suicide led by Madelin. All of the counselors were special in their own certain way, but Maddie was the most beneficial for me personally. She has the ability to make you feel better about yourself. She can make you feel comfortable when you are uncomfortable. She can inspire you when you feel uninspired. She can strengthen you when you feel weak. She can break down the insecure illusions you have about yourself and help you to see the truth about yourself. Maddie is one of the best counselors I have ever been around.

At this point in time, I would say the largest emotion I had was fear. I was scared for many different reasons. I was scared I would be a horrible counselor. I was scared I would make Joan and Aila look stupid for selecting me. Simply put, I was scared I would fuck up and be a fuck up. Maddie shut me up in my mind and calmed all of my fears. She made me understand that I would be a good counselor, and that I have already helped someone just by attending the training. Her encouraging words and faith in all of us made me realize that I *can* help survivors and make a difference in their lives. I believed I could be a good addition to THP, and I believed I could play a positive role in part of the healing process for people. My fears went away and I felt stronger and more confident.

The day continued with a presentation by a local detective who talked to us about the Sexual Assault Unit at the police department. After that, we then learned about legal issues and legal advocacy, followed by a training on domestic violence. Our last training was on lesbian, gay, bi-sexual, and transgendered (LGBT) survivors, and then we ended the day with another check-out question.

As usual, the fourth day started with a check-in question. The first training of the morning focused on working with adolescents and the second was on supporting significant others. After lunch, we had a three-hour training on childhood sexual abuse and incest. This turned out to be the most disturbing for me to hear. It was very difficult to listen to. I thought I would throw up on myself while contemplating the fact that some children are sexually abused. Thankfully, we ended the day on meditation and breathing exercises. Both were severely needed for all of us because the material we had just listened to was the hardest to deal with. The exercises worked for me and other volunteers I spoke to. I walked out of there happy and relaxed as opposed to depressed and angry.

The fifth and final day started off again with a check-in question. We then received a training on SANE nurses and evidence collection. SANE stands for "Sexual Assault Nurse Examiner". SANE nurses are specifically trained to adequately treat rape survivors. Some survivors are treated horrendously and blamed while being in a hospital, so I think it is vital that trained professionals treat survivors, should they choose to go to a hospital. THP does not force anyone to do anything. The choice is solely up to the survivor.

After our morning break, we were introduced to a survivor speaker and listened to her share her story. This turned out to be the most memorable experience for me throughout the whole week of training. There was nothing quite like hearing a survivor share her own story in her own words. While listening, I learned about the awful thing that happened to her and how it affected her life. I also learned that she has grown, and lives a very normal and functional life. I sat on the couch in awe of this woman as she calmly spoke and answered all of our questions. I thought to myself, *If she can experience rape and be strong enough to speak about it to others, then I believe anyone can.*

Overall, I loved the training and cared for all of my fellow volunteers with the work they would soon be doing. I felt a real connection to those around me and THP as an organization. I left the training thinking about what all of us had been through and accomplished together. I couldn't wait to start volunteering and looked forward to impacting those affected by sexual violence in a positive way.

That week of training was educational, intense, depressing, fun, and inspirational. I learned a lot. The more I listened, the more I learned and the more prepared I became. Some people in my life wondered how I could focus on sexual violence for a full week. Over time, more people have wondered how I even deal with working at a rape crisis center. They say things like, "Isn't it so depressing? How can you deal with that all day?" I think these are valid questions, but our training did not consist of misery for forty hours. In fact, THP is great at making you feel comfortable, helping you find coping skills, and offering support when needed. Volunteering at THP is not as depressing as one may think, mainly because THP staff and volunteers truly help people. What better gift is there to give and be given?

It may sound weird, but that one week meant so much to me. I've never done something like that in my life. I used to go to basketball camps, but all I did was play basketball. I've never been part of an organization whose sole purpose is to help anyone affected by sexual violence at no cost to them. To be in a room with so many people who cared about changing an evil in the world was special to me. I felt connected in a different way from anything I've felt before. I personally gained spiritual strength and growth. I believed the women I trained with, the staff and volunteers I have worked with, and anyone else who has done this work or contemplates doing this work is called to a purpose of prevention, education, and healing. It is a calling worth taking if you feel it inside.

Chapter 5

CASE MANAGEMENT

———

"Any reaction to an abnormal situation is normal."

Men were not allowed to work as hotline counselors or medical advocates when I first joined THP in 2007, so case management is the work that I did. I didn't even know what case management services were before I joined THP. I never thought about the financial losses survivors endure as a result of sexual violence. For some reason it never occurred to me. At the time, I was stuck on the violent aspect of the crime and all of the horrible aftermath. Finances or lack thereof did not enter into the equation for me. However, as nervous and uneducated as I seemed, I also realized I was one of the luckiest people at THP because I got to work directly with the case manager, Joan.

Joan and I first met when I interviewed for the internship. I remember praying that I would get the internship because I really wanted to volunteer at THP, but another part of me wanted the internship because I wanted to work with Joan. I enjoyed hearing Joan explain all that she does for survivors when we first met. I just loved being around her.

I quickly learned that Joan is a special person. Her kindness, empathy, patience, and listening skills are some of the best of anyone I know. I knew I had a lot to learn about case management and how to talk with survivors, and I knew Joan was one of the best people to learn from. I couldn't wait to team up with her and get to work.

I was nervous as hell when I started at THP and also learned that I was the second man to ever work in the THP office. It saddens me that I was only the second man to ever work in the THP office. There were a couple of male volunteers in the Community Outreach Department who had started this work before me, but I thought it was pathetic and unfortunate that only one other man worked in the office and only about six of us in total since the beginning of THP's existence. The majority of perpetrators are men, but the majority of men are not perpetrators. To all the men out there who are reading this: We have a responsibility in this issue and we need more men getting involved to help out in some kind of way. I believe it is imperative for more males to become involved in rape crisis work because it helps women and men. Some women begin to trust men again when they see that not all men are monsters. And men coming forward to get counseling increased because of the few men volunteering at THP. Guys, you have no idea how much it means to some people when they see a man care about this issue and try to do something about it.

The first couple of weeks at THP were spent learning about Joan's case management work and what my role would be. Joan taught me about what her job entails and explained what she wanted me to do. Initially, she did not have me speak to any clients. Joan wanted me to feel comfortable, which worked out great for me because I was not comfortable. I used to answer the phones, learn about financial resources, and organize the case management program. Speaking to clients did not become an option until I felt ready and knew what Joan actually does.

Joan works with survivors around housing and financial needs. She has brief consultations with them, which usually entail her answering questions about financial resource options as a result of sexual violence. She also assesses survivors' financial situations based on resources that are available, and explains where survivors can go to obtain other resources if necessary.

Safety is a huge concern for survivors, so Joan spends a lot of her time trying to help survivors with housing needs. Most survivors know their perpetrators, so safety in housing is critical. Joan helps with both immediate/emergency housing and long-term housing. She explained to me that domestic violence shelters are always a last resort, but necessary at times. Joan would rather send her clients to family or friends because she can never guarantee where someone will be placed. Survivors lose a great deal of control when they go to domestic violence shelters, which isn't always helpful when someone has already lost control from being raped against his or her will.

I would like to believe that anyone in need could go to a shelter and their life would be so much better, but that is not always reality. Joan explained to me that most clients do not go to DV shelters because of the lack of beds, or the area is too far from their job, therapist, or children's school. So what does Joan do when her clients do not want to go to a shelter, or can't get into one even though they live in fear? She validates their experiences. She is empathetic and provides the counseling that is needed. She will also tell her clients the system unfortunately sucks, and sadly, there just aren't enough resources.

Joan also helps her clients with moving expenses and long-term housing resources by working with housing specialists. She accompanies all survivors to appointments and will speak up for them if they have a hard time speaking for themselves. Joan does so much to try and meet the needs of her clients, but there are many obstacles. Long-term subsidized housing is difficult to acquire given the long waiting lists in the United States. Also, public housing authorities have certain preferences for rental assistance, and sexual assault is not one of them.

Finding alternate housing because of rape can be very difficult. Most survivors know their perpetrators, and the perpetrators may be controlling so much of their lives. For example, some of Joan's clients have spouses who raped them and control all of their finances. What do they do in that situation? Other clients of Joan's get evicted because their perpetrator stopped paying their rent. They cannot afford rent themselves, and therefore are left with the choice of being evicted or staying with their perpetrator.

There aren't many resources for survivors in these kinds of situations, so Joan educates her clients on other possible financial resources, such as public benefits, food stamps, disability, and cash assistance. Other aspects of case management involve helping survivors obtain victim's compensation, trying to obtain general resources for college students such as education grants, and helping with privacy concerns for college students.

I felt impressed and inspired by Joan's efforts. Over time, I felt ready to sit in on a call with a survivor. I'll never forget the moment when Joan called a woman and said, "Do you feel comfortable if a male volunteer listens in on this call with us?" I thought to myself, *Really? Did Joan really just ask that? Do women really not feel comfortable talking around me, even if I'm not saying anything and just listening? She can't even see me. She's just on the phone. Can she really not feel comfortable?* The answer is yes. Yes, there are women who do not feel comfortable talking when a man is present, even if he is on the phone and doesn't speak a word. And I had to accept that.

It is perfectly normal for some female rape survivors to not want to work with men. I also learned that this does not just pertain to women. There are men who would rather speak to a woman than a man. There are people who just don't feel comfortable speaking to certain people, and I think we should try to understand and support their decisions. I don't think we should judge or question, but rather empathize, listen, try to understand, and support in any way possible. The reality and intensity of working at a rape crisis center really hit me at that moment. To know that a woman does not feel comfortable speaking about anything related to her rape or her course of action going forward in her life proved to me how powerful the effects of this heinous crime really are to some people.

This particular woman did not mind that I listened to the conversation. She was raped in her apartment by a friend. I remember being horrified knowing that her friend could rape her, but I kept my comments to myself and listened. I thought to myself, *Do friends really rape their friends?* The answer is yes. Friends can rape their friends, partners can rape their partners, and family members can rape family members. I learned a very sad but important fact while volunteering at THP: Anyone can be raped or sexually assaulted, regardless of gender, age, ethnicity, religion, socio-economic status or sexual orientation.

I watched Joan in total admiration. She treated that woman with such kindness and gentleness. She listened to her, and allowed the survivor to speak, as opposed to telling her what to do or what to say. Joan simply listened, and I could see how effective and powerful that was for this particular woman's experience. As horrified as I was by all I had listened to, I learned a lot from that one conversation. Listening is one of the best things we can do for people, and I think it means a lot to survivors when we just listen to them. I learned a valuable lesson: Listen, validate, provide options, and support the one who is in need. This is how we can help others and play a positive, sometimes life-changing role.

All I cared about was helping others. But as passionate as I was, I was limited in the work that I could do, and I became frustrated by those limitations. In fact, I barely worked with clients while working in the THP office because most women did not feel comfortable working with me. It frustrated me, but it was something I had to accept. I just kept doing what staff asked me to do.

I came into THP one day and sadly learned that Joan's father had died. She flew to Ireland to attend her father's funeral and be with her family. I and everyone else at THP felt badly for Joan and her family. Obviously, it was an awful time for Joan. Everyone in the office thought about her and missed her. We didn't know how long she would be in Ireland for.

I couldn't help but think about Joan's clients while she was away. I decided to call them and let them know that Joan had had a family emergency, which was why they hadn't heard from her. I told them she would be back at some point, but I did not know when. I also told them I could help them if they felt comfortable speaking to a man. I didn't want Joan's clients to think she had forgotten about them, and I wanted to be able to help if someone needed it or if an emergency occurred.

One woman I spoke to did in fact feel comfortable speaking to me. She said, "I can't even believe I'm talking with you right now. I never would have been able to talk with you two months ago." However, not everyone was okay with me calling, and trying to help someone can also hurt someone.

There were many times that I thought more about THP than my actual job. My boss at the time supported my volunteer work with THP and was extremely flexible with my work schedule. He allowed me to leave the agency at a certain time to volunteer at THP, and I would make up my hours either at night or on the weekends. Occasionally, I would call clients from a conference room at the agency during my lunch break. So I continued to call Joan's clients, but from my job, not from the THP office. I will never forget what happened one afternoon when I called one of Joan's clients.

A woman picked up the phone and said, "Hello?" with very broken English. Her name is Veronika.

"Is Veronika there?" I asked.

I could barely make out her telling me that she was her.

I said, "Hi, my name is Bobby. I'm calling from The Healing Place. I work with Joan."

She immediately started speaking Russian. About fifteen seconds later a man came on the phone.

"Who is this?" he said sternly.

"Can I please speak with Veronika?" I responded.

"Who is this?"

"Can I just speak with Veronika?"

"What do you want?"

He sounded pissed off. I didn't know who he was. Given Veronika's file, I thought this man might have been her perpetrator. My mind started to race with questions and potential scenarios. I thought, *Is he her perpetra-*

tor? Is she safe? What do I do? What do I say? I didn't want to tell him that I was calling from THP. I couldn't tell him the reason for my call because she may not have told him, or anyone else in her life, about the rape. I also didn't want to endanger her, given that he might be her perp.

"This really won't take long. I just have to talk with Veronika briefly," I said.

"What the hell do you want!"

"Sir, can you put Veronika back on the phone?"

"Who the fuck are you!"

I was so confused and didn't know what to do. I decided to hang up. I figured the best thing was to just hang up and not piss this guy off anymore. I thought about Veronika all week. I didn't know what had happened, and didn't know if she was safe or not. *Did I just set off her rapist?* That situation was all I could think of for a week.

The following Monday I went into THP to volunteer. A clinician came in and said, "Bobby, there's a rapist at your job."

"What?" I responded, shocked. "There is? How do you figure?"

She said, "I spoke with Veronika, Joan's client. She said her rapist called her from your job. She's terrified. She hasn't been able to sleep in a week."

Some clinicians and staff members stood around us. I said, "I called Veronika from a conference room. I just tried to talk with her to tell her Joan will be gone for a while. Then some dude got on the phone and started getting pissed at me. I didn't know who he was so I hung up." It didn't hit us at first, but then it did. My voice had triggered Veronika. She thought I was her rapist. Everyone's mouth dropped.

Something like that had never happened at THP. I was devastated. I felt sick for a while. I couldn't believe that my voice could trigger such a horrible experience for someone, but it did. I never thought my voice could terrify a woman for a week and affect her sleep, but it did. I never thought trying to help in a simple way could turn out so badly, but it did.

The clinician called Veronika back and explained the situation, and thankfully Veronika no longer felt scared. Veronika was relieved. I was still in shock. I went home and pounded vodka by myself until I passed out in my living room chair.

I do not believe human beings fully understand the powerful effects of sexual trauma given our limited knowledge as finite beings. It is my opinion that even our medical professionals do not fully understand the powerful effects of sexual trauma. The brain is extremely intricate. As advanced as we are with our knowledge of the brain, we still know so little.

A female survivor once said to me, "I suffer in my soul." Another man once said to me, "You have no idea the anger I have in my soul." Given the limited knowledge we have about our brains and souls, I question why some people think they have all of the answers to what survivors should feel and do. It's great to offer knowledge and support, but those who may think they have all of the answers of what someone should do in a crisis may actually disempower and confuse that person.

Why do some people tell survivors to *get over it*? Why do some people say things like, "That happened two years ago, it's really time to move on"? Why do some people become angry at survivors when they are triggered? I pose these questions because I have heard them by many different people. These questions deter and sometimes cripple someone's growth and healing. If you get triggered, I want you to understand that you are not weak, crazy, or haven't *gotten over it*; you are normal. There is no timetable to grow and heal, and growth and healing is different for every survivor.

Sexual trauma can affect people in a variety of different ways, and people can easily be triggered or affected throughout different points in their lives. I have heard many absurd, illogical, and ignorant statements made to survivors about how they should *get over it*. I usually can't shut up when I hear certain statements. Depending on the situation, I ask some people, "Can you remember a good moment in your life? Do you remember your prom, your graduation, your wedding day, or the birth of your child?" They always say yes to something good in their life. I continue. "Imagine your wedding day. Do you remember your dress? The people? The music? The food? The weather? The dance floor?" They can always give me a vivid description of many things. I've heard people be able to describe the smell and taste of food they had twenty years ago. I continue. "So, if you can remember the smell of the steak twenty years ago, why can't a rape survivor remember a part of the rape two years ago? Why is it okay and normal to remember the smell of food, or the beautiful weather, or the song that people danced to, but rape survivors are weak if they remember a part of a horrific trauma? Why can people only remember good things, but can't remember the bad? I'm not saying people should dwell on the past, but why can't they at least remember part of it?" David Lisak writes:

> *The memory of a traumatic experience is not encoded in the same way as is a normal experience. The powerful neurochemicals that trigger the fight or flight response have far-reaching effects, including dramatic effects on the manner in which memories are encoded. Often, a traumatized person cannot generate the kind of narrative memory that we can normally muster for an important experience. Their memories are often fragmented, out of sequence, and filled with gaps. They may recall very specific details for particular aspects of the experience, and recall little or nothing for others. It is for this reason – the neurobiology of traumatic memory – that great care must be taken in interviewing trauma survivors. The fact that a traumatized person recalls a detail which they earlier had not is not prima facie evidence of fabrication; it is the characteristic way in which these types of memories are stored and recalled. The fact that they can recall the texture of the rapist's shirt, but cannot recall whether he was wearing a hat, is not evidence that something is being hidden; it is a product of how the brain encodes information during a trauma* (Lisak, 2002).

Megan had multiple experiences with sexual violence by multiple per-petrators. I once accompanied her for a speaking engagement at a college years after I worked as a case management intern. Megan told everyone in the room, "Any reaction to an abnormal situation is normal." This is a poem she wrote that I believe is fitting when thinking about triggers and the possible effects of sexual trauma. It is entitled *"no subject"*.

[no subject]

(no subject) emails terrify me.
Half seeing him in a person I half see as I walk the city streets
leaves me breathless and weak
And I wonder who gave him this power
Because, certainly, I did not.
At least, I don't remember doing it.
Perhaps between the I love yous
and the million things that got put aside for him.
Perhaps somewhere stuck among the silent grimaces
and the way my life molded around him.
Perhaps therein lies the power he holds.
Perhaps he knows he holds this power over me
As he moves through his life in this place and that
Doing all of the things, being all of the people
And moving along as if I never
existed.
Because that's what he wanted in the first place
Is it not?
A year ago.
This shouldn't ache
a year later.
It shouldn't force me under covers
and into dark rooms.
Shouldn't make me fear my own shadow

as I carry on the life that I somehow happily built
Before this came knocking again.
Again.
And it aches. It rips and roars through me
with the sound of a sobbing, hopeless little girl
who wants only for the pain to stop.
She needn't understand -
sin como, sin cuando ni de donde -
Just that it should stop now.
As she crouches beneath the covers
Her forehead sweaty with the tears and the heat
of a summer night beating on the blanket
asking her to come out and play.
Come out and play.
Come out and PLAY!
COME OUT AND PLAY!
A demand now.
And all she wants is sleep
Sweet, glorious sleep

If you are a survivor and get triggered, I want you to understand that you are more normal than you think. I have received many rape disclosures throughout my life by both men and women of different ethnicities and ages, and I can tell you survivors can easily get triggered at different points in their lives. Are people weak because they become triggered and still have painful memories? No. They are normal for having the reactions and memories they have. They are the ones who unfortunately have had to endure horrific trauma. Why do others tell them they shouldn't remember and just *get over it*? What does *getting over it* even mean?

I never spoke to Veronika again, and I stopped calling Joan's clients after that incident. I continued to work, but was limited in what I could do. I wanted to do more in the office, so I asked if I could help out with the Legal Department. The Legal Department had more clients than case management had and needed the help, so I thought it would be perfect. Turns out there were a lot more women who felt comfortable working with me while I helped with legal cases. The legal cases also allowed me to work with more men. These men usually called on behalf of their female partners. One story I remember was of a man who spoke with me because his girlfriend could not. I thought he might break down bawling after every sentence. Sexual violence not only affects a survivor; it affects his or her loved ones as well.

For nine months, I was blessed to be able to work under the direct supervision of Joan as a case management intern. While nine months may seem like a short amount of time in the grand scheme of life, the lessons I learned and the experiences I had changed my life for the better. Joan is a special person. She taught me how to be a better listener, counselor, advocate, and human being. Her passion for helping survivors is truly inspiring. She loves her job and continues to look for ways to do more meaningful things for survivors.

Chapter 6

OUTREACH & EDUCATION

———

"She said she never told anyone before, which means she has been keeping that all to herself for years."

The original agreement was for me to be an intern for a year, but I was frustrated by the lack of work and felt that I was not contributing as much as I would have liked to. I sat in the office with nothing to do for periods of time because most women did not want to, or could not speak with me. It is hard for me to be at a job and not work, no matter which work environment I am in. Not only did I feel discouraged, but I was emotionally drained. THP fulfilled me, but it affected my mind, heart, and soul. I loved being there; however, I needed a break. THP stresses the importance of "self-care", which was something I didn't often do and desperately needed. I decided to stop my internship three months earlier than we had discussed because this is what I had to do at the time.

THP had a goodbye meeting for me and the other interns who ended their internships at the same time. It was very sad and emotional because all of the interns had formed relationships with staff and each other. The staff also took us out for a farewell goodbye dinner, where they gave us plaques for the work that we had done. It was a beautiful end to our time in the THP office.

My internship ended, but I knew deep within that my work at THP would continue at some point in time. I needed a break, but it was only a matter of time before I got back involved. It's kind of hard to explain this, but I could not walk away from THP. Working at THP did not leave me. I didn't forget it. It changed me for the better. It became a part of me, and I became a part of it.

I stayed in touch with Joan, Aila, and others at THP over time. Even though I was no longer an "official" volunteer, I occasionally visited the office and talked about THP to people around me. People I met or knew still disclosed their stories to me, or sometimes people would ask about which services were available. I always sent everyone to THP if they needed help or had questions. I also raised money every year for THP's annual fundraiser. My siblings, parents, relatives, friends, and co-workers donated generously to my page every year. I raised over $2,000 every year solely due to the generosity and kindness of others.

At the time, Laureen was the boss of the Outreach and Education Department. She and I had many discussions in the office about sexual violence. We discussed strategies on how to prevent this crime and how we could educate different communities. She must have seen my passion and recognized something I did not see in myself because she always told me I would be great in O & E. She believed in my speaking skills when I did not believe in my speaking skills. She believed in my teaching skills when I did not believe in my teaching skills. She wanted me to join O & E, and she is the only one who even gave me the idea to join.

I knew I wanted to get back involved with THP, but I wasn't sure how. I never thought I would join O & E because I thought I would be a horrible public speaker. I didn't think I spoke too eloquently and I hated public speaking. The course I hated most in college was a required public speaking course, so the thought of being a public speaker seemed absurd. But I cared and I knew my work was not done. After deep contemplation,

I decided to say "fuck it" again. I called Laureen and said I would like to be a part of the O & E team if she would allow me. She easily and excitedly welcomed me into the group.

My first day in O & E consisted of a short training, followed by a meeting led by Laureen. I learned that O & E volunteers travel throughout different communities and facilitate prevention and educational workshops about sexual violence. O & E volunteers train some college Resident Assistants and accompany survivor speakers, which is when a survivor shares his or her story with people. Also, O & E volunteers table community health events and provide the public with THP information.

O & E volunteers are the face of THP to the larger community. They plant a seed in people's minds about the organization and the services THP offers. They teach, listen, empower, motivate, heal, and bring the existence of THP to people who do not know THP exists. I loved what they do because I believe traveling into different communities is very important in spreading the word. I also loved the fact that O & E volunteers heal in the streets. They never know what comes up for people when speaking or just sitting at a table with information about sexual violence. People can and do get triggered, so O & E volunteers have to be able to react to anything.

As usual, I felt nervous as hell. I did not know what I had gotten myself into, and I thought I would be a horrible public speaker. I did not have much confidence in myself or my speaking abilities, but I tried my best to believe in Laureen's words about me and gain a little confidence. As insecure as I was, I knew that I had something to offer. Deep down inside, I believed that my experience in the office working directly with survivors and significant others would benefit the team and the public with whom I would soon be interacting. That turned out to be true.

My first O & E engagement turned out to be a great learning experience, but also very intense and sad. Laureen and another volunteer co-facilitated a training to college RAs. This was my first time at an O & E speaking engagement, so my role was to sit back, observe, and learn. Thankfully I got to learn from Laureen.

As soon as I walked into the classroom I could see a woman looking very uncomfortable. She did not look happy or even content, and her leg could not stop shaking. Most of the students seemed to be fine, but this woman did not appear comfortable throughout the whole engagement. Another student, a man, had tears in his eyes.

About halfway through the engagement, a woman left the room. I noticed right away and thought something must be wrong. I was freaking out in my own mind. *Is she okay? Should I go out there? What is wrong! Dude relax, she might just be getting water or using the bathroom. Chill out.* Five minutes went by. I didn't know what to do. Thankfully, the other volunteer went out to check on her. They were both gone for at least a half hour. Laureen continued as if nothing had happened. She facilitated a difficult workshop like a true professional by herself. The woman eventually came back with Laureen's co-facilitator and seemed to be doing just fine. I asked her if she was okay. She smiled and said, "Yes."

This engagement taught me some valuable lessons. First, both Laureen and her co-facilitator taught me how to speak to an audience about such a difficult topic. They were articulate, intelligent, confident, and very personable. They connected with their audience. Second, I learned that people can become extremely emotional while listening to anything that has to do with sexual violence. Third, I learned that some people leave the room, and that an O & E volunteer should try to attend to that person and give them whatever help they may need at the time.

My first tabling experience to provide the public with information occurred at a festival outdoors. It turned out to be uneventful. We barely had anyone come over to the table. Some politician running for office came over to our table to speak about her campaign and how she cares about violence against women, but for some reason she didn't even care to ask about what THP does for women and men. Throughout the day, I noticed a young girl look over to our table multiple times. I wanted to walk over to her and give her a THP brochure, but I didn't know if her family was around or if she even wanted to interact with me. I made the best decision by staying away because I didn't believe this young girl was ready to hear about THP at the time, even though she was curious and kept looking.

Facilitating educational workshops and tabling community health events can be fun, exciting, boring, depressing, and life-changing. I have had many good and bad experiences while traveling into different communities as a THP volunteer. Bad experiences include organizers who keep us separated from the crowd, language barriers, and seeing people become triggered and cry. It's not an easy job to talk about such a sensitive issue as rape is, and the discussions, cards, and brochures do ignite many different kinds of emotions and sometimes painful memories.

No matter how many bad experiences I have had, the good has far outweighed the bad. I have truly had insightful, educational, and spiritual experiences while being a THP volunteer. People thank O & E volunteers for the work they do. The people smile. They grow. We laugh together and we have fun.

Some of my favorite times are when someone discloses for the first time. For example, a woman came up to the table early one morning at a farmer's market and asked us what we do. We told her that we were from THP, and then explained what THP and O & E does. She had never heard of THP. This particular woman became emotional and disclosed to us that she had been raped many years ago. She said she had never told anyone before, which meant she had been keeping that all to herself for years. I asked this woman if she wanted to talk. She did not want to, but she seemed relieved that she had disclosed to people who listened to her and who cared. I told her that we would be sitting at the table for hours, so she could come back to us if she wanted to. She thanked us for the work we did and left to check out the rest of the farmer's market. She never came back, but it was a special moment.

Being a part of O & E has allowed me to interact with, learn from, teach, and help a lot of people from different walks of life. Simply put, it's been a blessing for me. I have truly been blessed and I try my best to share my blessings with others. There have been ups and downs over the years, but I wouldn't change my experiences for anything in the world. Being present in the community and teaching and interacting with others is incredibly important. I hope that more people become community activists because that is one of the ways we can create real social change.

Chapter 7

REBECCA

———

"I didn't tell you my story to get sympathy; I told you my story to show you that it does happen."

Some of the most memorable moments for me as an O & E volunteer have been when I accompanied survivor speakers at a particular college for two consecutive years. The first year's event barely had any participants when I accompanied Megan. Only six of us were standing in the freezing cold, walking up and down streets, talking about sexual violence. There were more dogs walking around us than people who attended. It was small yet emotional and beneficial. Towards the end of the event, Rebecca, for the first time in her life, bravely shared her story with us. This was the first time she had ever read her story to a group of people, and it was the first time her school ever had this particular event.

Rebecca spoke again the next year to about fifteen people. The event took place in doors, and clearly, there were more people than the previous year. The night started with me speaking about THP's services. I then sat down while Alexis stood up to speak. After Alexis finished and answered questions from the students, Corey stood up to speak. After Corey answered questions, another student shared her story, and then other students read stories of other survivors. Towards the end, as in the previous year, Rebecca was the last speaker. This is Rebecca's story:

Becca: This is only the second time that I've told my story to a group of people, so please bear with me if my voice shakes...

Just about everyone knows the statistic people tell you before you head off to college that one in four college women will become a victim of sexual violence before she graduates. On December 2, 2010, before I'd even finished my first semester of my freshmen year, I became that statistic. What no one told me about that statistic was that it wasn't the creepy man in the bushes that I couldn't see coming that I had to worry about; it was someone I saw to be a friend that I had to worry about.

That night was supposed to be a relaxed night drinking and listening to music with a bunch of kids from my floor. But what really happened was a friend of mine who lived two doors down followed me into another room in my suite and started jokingly trying to tickle me. I told him to stop, and when he didn't, I went into my suitemate's room thinking that he would get the hint when I went in there to talk to her. But when I walked in, she wasn't there.

He came up behind me and trapped my arms at my side while he forced his hands down my pants and up my shirt. I couldn't tell you how long I was in there with him. I know it was only for a few minutes, but everything was happening in slow motion... it felt like forever...I finally broke free from him and ran away. I slammed the door to her room thinking, "If he's going to chase me, he's going to have to slow down long enough to open the door."

Now I think it's kind of funny how your brain works during trauma. It's funny that I couldn't tell you what was going through my head the rest of the time while I was in that room with him except that one phrase. He texted me afterwards and asked, "Where did you go?" and "I'm sorry if I went too far. I hope I didn't hurt your feelings."

I expected the people around me to be supportive of me. I mean, the whole floor of my dorm were criminal justice majors, so I thought they would believe me. I was dead wrong. My friends were supportive to begin with, but it didn't last long. People who were supportive to begin with wouldn't testify on my behalf at the school's misconduct hearing. I dropped the criminal case after the male special victim's unit detective on my case told me that a discrepancy in my statement versus his would mean that I would be torn apart on the witness stand. Before I left, the male detective said, "I hope you learned your lesson about how you should act towards male friends because not all of them are going to take joking around the same way."

To make matters worse, the school didn't have the hearing until mid-February, which would have been fine except they allowed him to continue living two doors down from me until then. During the second semester, I was diagnosed with acute trauma based depression and I suffered from the effects of post-traumatic stress disorder (PTSD). I came to realize that the fear I felt that night stemmed more from the terror at the helplessness of knowing I couldn't do anything about what was about to happen. Some people thought, "Why didn't you initially run or scream or fight?" Until that night I would have said the same thing as them, but when you're in that situation of being paralyzed by fear and shock, everything you said you would do goes out the window.

If I could go back and tell my freshmen year-self something, I would have told myself to be more careful and not let my guard down around anyone. I thought it was something that would never happen to me. But even more importantly, I would have told myself to keep my head held high against everyone at the school that didn't believe me and talked about me. I tried to hide myself whenever I was out around campus. I dressed in baggy clothes, and I hardly went out of my room. I would have told myself that it wasn't my fault and that no matter what anyone said, I didn't deserve what happened to me. It's easy to look back at a situation and say I should have done this and I should have done that, but what's more important is to look at what you do with the situation after the fact.

I didn't tell you my story to get sympathy; I told you my story to show you that it does happen. It's not just something that happens on TV. It really can happen to anyone. If you don't think about my story any time after today, please just remember this: If someone comes to you to tell you a story like mine, don't judge them and don't tell them you would have done something different. Just listen and give them support. Thank you.

All of the participants in the crowd stood up, formed a circle, and held candles after Rebecca finished sharing her story. Every person who stood in that circle had the opportunity to share any words they wanted or needed to share. Heartfelt words and deep appreciation for the night and the survivor speakers came out of many mouths. Plenty of tears strolled down many faces. It was one of the most intense experiences I have ever had as a THP volunteer.

Rebecca's boyfriend, Todd, drove from a different state to be a part of this event. He was the one who actually helped Rebecca after the sexual assault. While standing in our circle, be began to break down bawling in a way that I haven't seen from a man since I started at THP. We gave him a safe space to cry and allowed him to have as much time as he needed to say whatever he wanted to say. Todd could not understand how someone could sexually assault Rebecca, how she could be blamed for being sexually assaulted, and how she wasn't believed. He sat up with Rebecca for hours after her assault. He listened to her, talked with her, watched movies with her, and supported her in whatever way she needed at the time. I believe Todd's actions that night are examples of how to best support someone who has been sexually assaulted.

There is power in our words. There is often more power in our own voices than we can fathom. Rebecca proves what can happen when someone speaks up. Any student has the power to create an event at their school, empower others by speaking, give others a voice, and educate others in hopes of joining a cause. The first year, there were only six of us. The second year, there were fifteen of us. Who knows what the third year will bring. What about the fifth year? What about the twentieth year? How many other college students out there can do what Rebecca did?

Chapter 8

PUNK ROCK

———

"Today has been life changing."

A nother memorable experience for me as an O & E volunteer is when I signed up to facilitate a workshop at a three-day punk rock music festival. The proceeds of the shows would be given directly to THP. I jumped at the opportunity to work at this event as soon as I heard music was involved. One of my passions is music, so I was really excited about the engagement. I loved the idea of having an educational workshop before a live concert, and then staying throughout the day to provide resources and information to the fans and musicians. That particular weekend turned out to be very special.

The festival lasted three straight days and consisted of over forty punk and hardcore bands. On Friday night, bands played at a house party which I did not attend. On Saturday, the fest continued at a school, and the final day ended on Sunday in a different location. I was not sure how many people would show up at 3pm to have a discussion about sexual violence before ten plus bands poured their hearts and souls into their music, but I couldn't wait to find out.

I'd say there were about one hundred people who participated in the workshop/discussion. At the time, that was the most people I had ever spoken to. We did an exercise at the beginning of this particular workshop to help everyone understand how common sexual violence is. I asked the audience to stand up.

"Remain standing if you've heard the word *sexual harassment,*" I said.

Everyone stayed standing.

"Remain standing if you've heard the word *sexual assault.*"

Everyone stayed standing.

"Remain standing if you've heard the word *rape.*"

Everyone stayed standing.

"Remain standing if you've seen sex in the media."

Everyone stayed standing.

"Remain standing if you've seen violence in the media."

Everyone stayed standing.

"Remain standing if you've seen sexual violence in the media."

Everyone stayed standing.

"Remain standing if you know someone who has been affected by sexual assault."

Everyone stayed standing.

"Remain standing if you know someone who has been affected by rape."

One woman sat down.

"Everyone, look around," I said.

Everyone started to look around the gym at each other.

"Only one person sat down. I want everyone to look around and see there are that many people in this one gym who know of someone who has been raped. Think about that for a moment…I ask that you think about this for the next hour and a half while we continue on with the workshop. Thank you for doing this. You can now sit down."

I have done that exercise many times, but I have never seen that many people standing. This surprised me. It was very sad to see that many people stand and acknowledge that they know someone who has been raped. In one art school gym, ninety-nine out of one hundred people knew someone in their life that had been raped. What does that teach us? How common is this crime?

That experience got me thinking. *Have these people that they know of told anyone? If so, how were they treated? Were they treated poorly or blamed, or were they believed and offered compassion and support from the one they told? Have they sought out help or have they internalized? Do they speak or stay silent? How many of us know someone who has been raped? How are those people feeling inside? What do they think about themselves? How are we treating them? Do we even acknowledge or think about their pain? Are we helping them if they need help? What are we doing to attempt to prevent such vile crimes? Do we even care? If so, what are we doing about it? If not, how many more will suffer?*

I had dinner and drinks with Dave, a fellow O & E volunteer, a few weeks after the concert. Dave is another one of a kind person who teaches me a lot, keeps me motivated, and helps me to be a better facilitator and person. I didn't think it was possible to get excited about a presentation on consent, but he somehow managed to accomplish that goal. Dave is an incredibly gifted and passionate public speaker, facilitator, and healer, and he is an amazing asset to O & E.

Dave loves music as much as I do and we both play the guitar. I said to him, "Dude, come over some night. We can have some beer, play some music, and I'll teach you how to cook." We picked a night and I picked him up at his apartment. I drove him back to my apartment, guitar and amp in hand, and we had a few beers on my back deck. We started discussing THP and sexual violence as a problem throughout humanity. We talked about O & E and how we thought we could be a little more effective in our jobs. We discussed THP as an organization that we both love. I told Dave about the punk rock festival and about the exercise that we did.

"How many people do you think live on my street in all of these apartments?" I asked.

"I don't know. A lot," Dave responded.

"I'd say so. At least two hundred. Probably a lot more. How many people on this street that we are currently looking at have been affected by sexual violence? How many people have been raped, or know someone who has been raped? What do you think?"

"Probably a lot."

"I agree. How many people on this street know THP exists? What do you think?"

"Not many. Maybe none."

"I agree. How sad is that if that is true? Now, take that information to the next street over. How many people are on the next street over?"

"The same."

"Correct. And the next street? The same. What about all the people in this one city? How many people live in this small city? And how many people in this small city actually know that THP simply exists?"

"I don't know."

"Neither do I, but I don't think a lot know. Now take that throughout other parts of the city. How many people in the city have been raped or know someone who has been raped? How many people simply know THP exists?"

"I don't know."

"Neither do I, but I don't think a lot. Now what about the whole state? What about the country? What about the world? How many people in the world have been raped or know someone who has been raped, but do not know a rape crisis center in their area or surrounding area simply exists? How are people supposed to get help if they need it and they don't even know places like THP exist, or in areas that don't even have rape crisis centers? Can people seek help from friends, family members, or anyone else? Of course. But what if these people treat them poorly, or treat them well, but don't know how to help them? What if they want someone specifically trained in sexual violence? What are they to do? What are they doing now? What will they do in the future? And what about all the people throughout the world who do not live near a crisis center?"

Dave pondered the questions as we continued our night.

The exercise at the punk festival really stuck with me. As we continued on with the workshop, I noticed many faces in the crowd. Some seemed intrigued, some eager, some passionate, some nervous, and some had tears in their eyes. I remember one specific man in the crowd. I remember his whole being sitting in that chair. He sat there with his arms across his chest and hands in his arm pits, staring at me. His eyes seemed to penetrate me in a way that is hard to capture with words. It made me think of the very real possibility that this young man had never participated in a discussion like this, yet he may have wanted to or needed to for years. It broke my heart. He ended up following me later that night with tears in his eyes. He wanted to talk away from the crowd. He said, "Thank you so much." I told him he was welcome.

While walking down the street that night, a man I will never see again just said the words "Thank you". I have no idea what he has experienced in his life. I don't know if he is a survivor himself, or how he has been affected by sexual violence. And I don't know what the impact of that day has been on his life. But what I do know is he seemed relieved and happy. Tears can be quite healthy and freeing, and I believe they were for him that day.

His tears were tears of joy, I think, and he seemed appreciative of what THP did that day. I didn't want to push him to talk about anything serious, so I started talking to him about his life and his interests. He walked away with a smile, and hopefully a sense of peace. But what did I really do? Not much. All I did was get up, speak, stand behind a table, and listen to music. I just asked him simple questions about his life and his passions. Nothing too special, but to him it was. I think this story poses some questions. *What else can all of us do for others? How simple can it be to give another peace, even if it's for just a moment? But if it is for just a moment, can that peace last even longer?*

Throughout the day, there was one band that I enjoyed the most. I could hear their talent and feel their emotion as soon as I heard the first note. I enjoyed seeing them perform and express a part of themselves.

Their last song truly struck me. All four members of the band screamed something in unison. They yelled from the depths of their souls away from the microphones. I wondered what they were yelling. *What did it mean to them?*

I went over to where the guys from this band were standing because I wanted to compliment them and buy their cd if they had one.

"You guys sounded awesome. For real, you sounded sick. You're very talented," I said.

"Thanks man. We really appreciate that," they responded.

"Do you have a cd? I'd love to buy one."

"Are you serious?"

"Yeah dude. Hook me up."

"Cool man. It's two dollars."

"Are ya kiddin me? Dude, take a five."

"Are you serious? That's too much."

"No it isn't. Take it. Thanks for the cd."

I don't know how the act of me giving them $5 somehow blew them away, but it did. To me it was nothing. If anything, I made out because I got a new cd for five bucks. But to them it meant more.

I asked them what they thought of the workshop. All of them really enjoyed it. I asked them if they had learned anything and they said they had. It turns out they loved the workshop.

"It was awesome. I didn't expect to talk about sexual violence today. It's a really hard topic to hear. We've never had this before," one of them said.

"It is. But it's really important to listen to and engage in. People are hurting and might not have anywhere to go or know where to go."

"Sometimes all people need is just someone to listen to them."

"I agree."

"And there's A LOT of people that need someone to listen to them."

"I agree. It's really unfortunate, but I'm trying."

"You should travel and do this in other states."

"I'd love to, but I wouldn't even know where to begin. I think you should do this work in your state. Would you ever get involved where you live?"

"Yes, we definitely would."

One of the band members later said to me, "Today has been life changing."

The whole day was amazing. I really enjoyed some of the bands and felt like I got an education on punk music and the punk scene. I am thankful to all of the musicians and fans. A lot of the music is really intense, and some of the lyrics are about rape. I remember one singer in particular. She spoke in between songs, but I couldn't make out all that she said. I do however remember her saying, "Rape is real. Believe someone if they tell you." She is right. Rape is real, and some people experience some of the most disturbing things possible while others don't even believe them. Unreal experiences to some are real experiences to others.

Day three of the festival occurred at a smaller venue. I still participated in a workshop, but there were far less people. There were only about ten of us in a little room, but it was just as important to have. After the engagement, I stood at a table with more THP information for the rest of the day. I listened to more music and talked with people for hours. I loved it.

Some people came over and told me how much they respect me for the work I do at THP. I thanked them but told them I am nothing special. I always tell people I just give a fuck about the issue. I care and I made a choice. I asked them if they wanted to do this kind of work and they said yes. So I talked with them and helped break down the barriers that were keeping them from getting involved. Usually, the only thing keeping us from helping others is ourselves. I believe that once we understand that, we are then able to break the negativity and insecure illusions we may have about ourselves or our abilities.

I explained to them how hard it was for a twenty-two year old man to ask if he could volunteer at a place that helps people affected by sexual violence. I told them that I was nervous and scared, but I contemplated, prayed, and then said "fuck it". What was the result? I have helped many people in a variety of different ways. Also, my life has changed for the better. Would they want the same, if not more? I told them they can make even more of a difference than I can (and so can you if you want to). They understood, and they then put their names and contact information on our volunteer sign-up sheet.

The punks at this great three-day festival were kind enough to invite us back to have trainings and table the event the following year. They also kindly gave the proceeds of another three-day festival to THP. I remembered some of the people and some remembered me. I thanked them for having us back a second time. They were happy to have us back as well.

The musicians and fans made a great connection with THP. Together, we taught each other, raised thousands of dollars for the people THP helps, and changed some lives. I am so thankful to everyone who participated and those who gave any amount of money they could afford to support a great cause.

To all the punks who may be reading this, know that I cherish these memories and I keep all of you in my heart. I want to say to all of the bands and fans "good luck", and I wish you all the best with your music and lives. Love and peace. Be well.

-Bobby

Chapter 9

COREY

———

"The other reason that I pressed charges functionally is that I don't have any control over what he does, but the main thing to me was making sure that there was a record. So even though the verdict was completely not, to me "just", at least there is a paper record of what he did to me."

All survivor speaker accompaniments are intense for the survivors and O & E volunteers, but one very unique and powerful event occurred when I accompanied Corey at a rally. I emailed Corey to meet before the engagement, as I do before all survivor speaker engagements, so we could become acquainted with each other and form a game plan. Corey immediately wrote back, and we decided to grab lunch. While eating, Corey told me his story. His story is obviously sad, but I was truly horrified to learn that his perpetrator accepted a plea bargain for probation of two years and a $250 fine.

Corey is a very soft spoken person, yet I could feel his passion when he spoke. After listening to his story and learning about the pathetic sentence that his perpetrator received, I felt compelled to ask if he would be willing to share his story for this book. Without hesitation, Corey agreed, but the rally kept our focus.

We met each other an hour before the march began. About two hundred people came out for the three hour march to help play a role in "ending rape culture". The organizers of the rally were extremely disorganized and didn't even get a permit, so Corey did not have permission to use a microphone. This pissed me off because his story is not something that is meant to be screamed. Thankfully, they gave him a megaphone. My anger continued once Corey started speaking because instead of listening to him, people talked and laughed. I thought it was ridiculous that these people came to a rally to "end rape culture", whatever that even meant, and didn't even have the decency to just shut up and listen to the most important and effective speaker throughout the whole day.

Corey spoke honestly and passionately, and he captivated the audience. It is hard to explain the look on the people's faces, but the eyes of most of the people stayed fixated on Corey. In my opinion, the majority of the two hundred people were engaged, disgusted, horrified, saddened, impressed, and empowered by Corey's speech. The people began to scream and chant once Corey finished, and then the march began through the streets. Throughout the day, people came and spoke to Corey offering kind words and appreciation. He connected to the people.

After the rally, Corey said he wanted to record his story for this book, so we made plans for him to come to my apartment the next week for dinner. While having a few drinks over chicken parmesan and penne, Corey and I got to know each other a little more. I learned that Corey grew up in the Midwest and has been living on the east coast for over a decade. Corey looks like a woman, but identifies as a man, which I did not understand. Corey explained to me that he is transgender. For him, this means that while he was born and raised as a girl, he now lives his adult life as a trans guy.

I had only known Corey at that point for two weeks, but in that short amount of time we developed a strong connection. Corey is one of a kind and I am thankful that I have met him. His words matter, and his story, as with all of the survivors, should be told and spread. We started recording after dinner. This is Corey's story:

Corey: I'm glad to be a part of this project. I think it's really important. I'm going to try to answer questions and just talk about things. This is all my opinion and coming from my perspective of being a multiple sexual assault survivor. It's been ten and eleven years since both assaults. I think if you had interviewed me ten or eleven years ago, it would be an entirely different interview. But now I'm coming from a perspective where I really do feel like when we're talking about healing, and we're talking about things like being a survivor of sexual violence long-term, time really is the main thing. I don't really believe that you're ever healed from something like that because it leaves a mark on you, just like anything traumatic that you experience in your life. But I do believe in healing, and also in the power of transformation.

I'm going to use the name of the perpetrator that I use in my speeches. I'm going to refer to "Bill" as Bill, but like you saw in the documents, his name is not Bill. I call him Bill because if I said his name during a speaking engagement, it might actually trigger me. It's one of those weird things. Someone will just say his name regularly, completely out of context, and I get triggered. So I like to refer to him as Bill.

Before I talk about Bill, I want to mention the first time I was assaulted. I was terrified at the time. The guy basically tried all night to rape me. I'm not sure whether he did or not because I was so afraid of him that I actually completely disassociated most of the time, but I do remember him and his weight being on top of me. When he wasn't, I just kept saying, "I want to sleep." I didn't say no, and later I kind of used that to think that I wasn't sexually assaulted because I didn't say no. But in the meantime when he wasn't trying to have sex with me even though I didn't say I didn't want to, he was holding me so tightly that it actually hurt my skin. It was a very intense experience.

Afterwards, the guy called me and said, "I'll give you anything. What can I do? What do you want? I'm sorry. Whatever I did I'll make it up to you." What I could do at the time was change my number. I don't think he actually gave me his real name, but I gave what I knew to be the name that he used, and his phone number, and a description of what he looked like to campus security. That was the best I could do. I did not press charges because I was very afraid of him.

That summer, I traveled to Philadelphia and moved in with Bill. I wanted so deeply and desperately to transform that experience in Massachusetts and do something positive. So I took an internship at an organization that worked to educate people about sexual assault. I wanted to reach out and support people who had this experience by doing this internship. Things were going okay for me. Everything seemed to be working out okay (it wasn't perfect but it was okay) for me, but Bill started to change over time.

It started off with hugging. That was the first thing. I noticed that when he hugged me it was increasingly longer and it felt intimate, but not from my end. After a while, I actually had to talk to him and I said, "Can you please not hug me so much?" I didn't say it made me uncomfortable because I was trying to be nice, which I regret. Not that I think that me doing that was the cause of anything, but I still have some hard feelings towards him. He would also make comments like, "If it gets too hot in your room you can come sleep in my bed." That was really inappropriate. I was like, "No, I'm not going to do that."

I'm really into charity and volunteering. I always have been. One time we went on our trip to the Poconos to drop off toys for needy kids. He said something to the effect of, "I have some sort of urinary issue, and in an emergency, I might need you to hold my penis to help me pee." I was just like, "Well, I'm not going to do that."

Me: He said that on a trip when you were giving gifts to needy kids?

Corey: Yeah. In the Poconos. It was through his church. They were needy kids. THAT was legit as far as I could tell. I really believe this because I felt it at the time and I still feel it: part of the issue is that I didn't want to believe he was capable of doing these things. When I felt uneasy about things he did, I actually doubted myself because in my head I said, "He's a nice guy. He's my friend. He's a good guy. Because I was assaulted before, I'm being overly critical of him." I actually doubted myself more than I doubted him, which is a strange thing, but I was in denial because I didn't want to believe that he was capable of doing something like that. I wanted to believe that he was my friend and he would respect me. He did a good job of indicating that he would, or at least convincing me that he would because every time he did something inappropriate, he responded and said the right things and stopped.

We went to an art museum in Philadelphia together. We went to a famous outdoor garden with sculpted trees and fountains together. But to me, none of this had any sort of a romantic context. I had never been to Philly and I wanted to explore the city.

Bill at the time was fifty-eight. He is now sixty-eight. He was a good five years older than my dad. There was no way that I could possibly sexualize him in any way. But Bill took his hand, non-consensually, and put it down my shirt and started touching my chest. The next morning, he exposed his genitals to me.

In some ways that was just unbelievable to me because it was like a boiling pan. It was like the heat had gone on so high and everything was going so fast that I couldn't even…it was nuts to me. It was like standing on a train track and the train is coming, and you know the train is coming, but just the shock of everything that was happening was so crazy to me.

Bill was an older gentleman. He did a really good job of portraying himself as a nice guy, as a religious guy, as a real generous, down to earth guy. Unfortunately that was a mask. At least when it came to me, the guy he was is the guy that betrayed my trust and used that trust to sexually assault and expose his genitals to me.

I trusted Bill. I thought he was a friend. I explained what had happened to me in Massachusetts, and instead of honoring that, he sexually assaulted me and he used that as an excuse to justify it. He justified himself by saying, "I wanted to get you used to being touched by a man." What the fuck does that have to do with anything? You wanted to help me get over the fact that I was sexually abused by sexually abusing me? That totally makes sense, except not at all and it's completely disgusting and ridiculous.

I'm not saying that this is the right response but I really felt like on top of being sexually assaulted, the primary issue with what Bill did to me was that he violated our friendship; a friendship that I valued. He also violated my consent, but to me, the fact that I knew him and trusted him made it harder than when I was sexually assaulted by a stranger that I didn't know. In some ways while it wasn't easy, it was easier because it wasn't somebody that I had any affinity to. When you trust somebody, when you really tell someone intimate details about your life, spend time with them, and open yourself up, and they violate that trust, it's like another layer. It's another thing.

When I decided to file a police report, the detective kept saying, "Why are you angry?" It was kind of like, "I don't understand what isn't clear. I'm telling you that my roommate who I was friends with touched me not consensually, and then in the morning he exposed himself to me to show me that he was not sexually attracted to me. What is okay about that? What about that is normalizing?" Nothing. But I feel like under the guise of…I feel like under the guise of…No. Fuck that. I feel like what the detective was trying to do was establish if I was telling the truth or not.

Me: The detective was trying to do that?

Corey: Yeah. He was trying to understand if we had dated and were lovers.

Me: Do you mind if I ask what questions he asked? Do you remember?

Corey: I can give a rough sketch of what he said. This was ten years ago so it's not going to be verbatim, but he was basically asking if we had ever had sex, if we were lovers, if we had ever dated. Things like that. Sort of along the lines of, "Did you do anything that would suggest to him that it would be okay to touch you?" How do you answer a question like that? What I said to the detective, and in court, was that I only viewed Bill as a friend. But in fact I had told Bill that I did not want a sexual relationship with him (or anyone else). After having been sexually assaulted that winter, I wasn't in a place where sex felt safe.

This is something that I don't always talk about in my speech, but I will mention because we're having a more in-depth discussion. When you testify and when you go to court, people ask you all these questions. What they didn't take into account is how incredibly hard it is to talk about it. My mother was in court when I testified. My dad was not very much in the picture. I was sitting there in court with my mother who raised me, talking about how someone who is older than she is exposing his genitals to me to let me know that he was not sexually attracted to me. Do you know how crazy that is? It was surreal.

Basically in that situation he didn't have to testify. I had to testify. If I didn't testify, they probably would have thrown out the case. Did I want to testify? Oh my God no. If I think about it too much I'll probably get sick just thinking about it because it was so...it was so stressful. All of the burden was on me. A crime has been committed against me, and all the weight to show that it happened is on me.

Then you add to the fact that this guy was smiling the whole time. He was smiling like he won the lottery. He didn't stop smiling at all. He was smiling while I was talking about how he sexually assaulted and exposed himself to me. It was like a movie. It was surreal that my testimony is being recorded to decide whether they are going to press charges, and I'm facing this guy who sexually assaulted me, and he is smiling at me. It's unfathomable. It's like, "You have no understanding. You have no understanding."

I don't believe in suicide fundamentally or spiritually, but after it happened, it was probably the lowest point in my life. For me I feel like I have healed a lot, but I was REALLY angry afterwards. There were times when I didn't feel like living. I didn't feel like killing myself, but I just felt so...I had already been sexually assaulted. Bill knew that I had been sexually assaulted because one night after he was helping me with my computer he touched the back of my leg. I said to him, "You know, the reason why I'm doing this internship is because...." and I told him what had happened in Massachusetts.

I did not want to press charges just because I knew how it's pretty clear there's a pretty good, well-established notion that if you've been sexually assaulted it's very difficult to press charges and testify. It's relative, but for me...

Me: It is hard. That's why many people don't.

Corey: I felt like I was the one on trial. I didn't feel like he was on trial. I felt like he got to just sit there and smile at me and I'm the one that had to talk about what happened. I used the word "molest" for a lack of a better word. He molested me and exposed himself to me. That is totally fair and balanced, right? That is totally just. No, it's not. People often say if you've been sexually assaulted, go to the police.

Me: Do you think he knew that he was going to plea bargain? Given potentially the pathetic punishment?

Corey: Yup. Of course he knew. I said to the prosecutor, "If he doesn't admit guilt, please try to put him in jail because he will do this to someone else." Of course he would plea bargain. It made sense because it was a misdemeanor. What he did to me was a misdemeanor.

Me: By the law in Pennsylvania.

Corey: By the law in Pennsylvania. Not obviously on its impact on my life. He was charged with three things. He was charged with harassment. He was charged with indecent exposure, which was him exposing his genitals to me. He was charged with indecent assault, in a misdemeanor way. The harassment was thrown out. In legal terms, they said that they couldn't fully prove that he exposed himself to me, even though I testified that he exposed himself to me, but apparently there was some minor detail I didn't get right. I don't know.

He got the maximum sentence, which in Pennsylvania at the time, and I think still currently, is two years probation. Also, on top of that totally inconsequential sentence compared to the maximum sentence I'm living with, he was also fined $250 to the state, which doesn't make any sense to me but whatever. I'm guessing it was to cover legal fees or something. I don't know. I'm not a lawyer. But that is just ridiculous to me. And then also during his probation only, he couldn't rent out his house to anybody. Now he can, which sickens me.

Me: And he continues to pursue his Christian ministry out of his home?

Corey: I went on his website the day that I looked up the verdict. He does Christian counseling for people with troubled marriages and other people who need it. On his website it lists all the things he does in the house that he sexually assaulted me in. So people are coming to this house that I rented a room from him in, and getting counseling from him.

The other reason that I pressed charges functionally is that I don't have any control over what he does, but the main thing to me was making sure that there was a record. So even though the verdict was completely not, to me "just", at least there is a paper record of what he did to me. And that if he does try to do that to someone else, that there is an established record that he did this to me. And that he pled guilty. It's minor victories. I feel good about it. I feel good about my decision to press charges. I just feel like the system is not equal. My hope is maybe that it's gotten a little bit better, but at least in 2002 I found it to be a very frustrating, very fragmented system.

There were resources I could have gotten that I didn't know were available. It was not about me in a good way. It was about me providing evidence of what he did to me so that there could be at least a preliminary hearing. There could be criminal charges and what he would get charged with, but besides that, I did not find it empowering and I did not find it to be a system that was set up to be supportive and help me through the process. I feel like the only thing that helped me through the process was that I was so angry and frustrated that that had happened and also concerned that it could have happened to someone else. That was what drove me. That anger and frustration and pain was the impetus, but if anything, the criminal process was more of a barrier for justice than it was a bastion. I know that's a fancy word but seriously.

The crime shows are like, "You're guilty of murder. You get the full sentence." I like to watch those shows. I like when the bad guy goes away. But it's not always that story. That story is sometimes just a story. If Bill had just punched me, or done some other non-sexual crime, I feel like it would have been a whole different thing. But because of the sexual nature of the crime, there was some subtext of, "What did I do to bring this upon myself?" And the answer was to the best of my ability, I tried to communicate every way I could that he did not have my consent because he didn't. There wasn't anything I did to bring it upon myself. I was in his proximity. That was it.

Me: There was nothing you did to bring it upon yourself.

Corey: Nope.

Me: He is also an intelligent man, right? There was a huge age differential and he knew what he was doing. Would you agree?

Corey: Oh yeah. It's hard for me to say this because it's hard for me to think about, but I felt pretty certain that he had done this to someone before me. There's no certainty because there weren't any documented cases, but I just had a feeling that how he established trust with me and how he was, and how he always knew how to say the right thing when he did cross a boundary. Even if he hadn't, I know he could so easily…SO EASILY do that to someone else.

It's still painful.…ten years of my life…it's still painful… sometimes I have nightmares about it. I've had nightmares about him. I think it is somewhat helpful for me to look at legal documents and think about it, but in other ways it brings up those old painful feel-

ings. It's a mixed bag. There's a part of me that still feels that anger and frustration towards him.

I forgave him because it was about me. I haven't forgotten what he has done and I haven't completely let go, but I was so angry for several years. I needed to get to the point where I just let go of that. It wasn't about him. It wasn't about condoning what he did. It was just about me getting to the point where I could turn the corner and say, "Yes, what happened really did have a huge detrimental, negative, hurtful, and emotionally painful effect on my life, but I can't sit in that forever because I didn't choose to be in that place and I can't stay in that place." Bill: I don't forgive you because of you. I forgive you because I need to start changing directions.

I really did believe that doing that internship would help transform that scary experience I had. I don't think it actually did, but that was my hope. I was a very optimistic and hopeful person.

Me: That's the beauty of you. You still have it. That's a good thing.

Corey: I think I'm a little more cautious and reserved. People say to me sometimes, "You have a wall up." And I say, "Yeah, I'm doing okay. I'm slowly chipping away, but yeah, I will have a wall up for a while."

Me: The optimism is still inside of you. You just spoke at a rally in front of two hundred people.

Corey: I just lock it up a little tighter. It's still there.

Me: It's still burning inside of you.

Corey: It's a little more guarded because when you trust somebody that much, when you tell somebody things about your life that you don't really tell people, and you have that vulnerability, and you really share with them, that is...I don't know about anybody else, but I was not raised in a touchy feely emotional family. I was friendly and trusting, but I have never been super, "Let's talk about our feelings", because that wasn't the culture of my family. So when I did open up, and when I did let down those barriers, it was a huge deal. It meant that I really trusted and cared about you. So to me in some ways that was harder for me. Obviously, being sexually assaulted was hard, but it was that I really trusted him and let him in. That made it worse to me.

There was a period after that where I did not trust anybody. I didn't care what they were selling, how nice and wonderful they were, I just didn't trust anybody. I just couldn't. It was a loss. It was a loss of that part of me that had been so open, so generous, and so trusting that I just said, "Fuck it. I am not going to trust anybody. I don't care what they say. I can't trust it. They might say all the right things and then use it against me or hurt me." There was a long period when I didn't let anybody in.

When I tell my story, I do not talk about my family much, but after I left the internship I came home. So I come home and I'm a total mess. Emotionally I was a total mess. I feel like what happened was that my mom couldn't process what happened to me, so instead, because she couldn't deal with it, she would say things like, "I don't want to talk about it." Or years later she would say, "I don't want to bring it up. Get over it. That was a bad summer for everyone including you." No mom: I was sexually assaulted. I wouldn't call that a bad summer. I didn't choose to get sexually assaulted, but had to deal with the effects it had on me.

I wish I could say that my parents were supportive. My mom did go to the hearing and actually she was pretty good. But before that there was a period of maybe two months where everyone acted like I was completely irrational. I just had this terrible, traumatic, awful thing happen to me, and everyone seemed to be acting like it didn't happen. But I could not pretend it didn't happen because it was completely affecting my life. I don't want to be angry. But I was angry because I feel like I was sinking under the weight of this and nobody was acknowledging it or being supportive.

Me: I've only known you for two weeks, but I do not think you are an angry person. When I look at you and I hear you, the last thing I think of is that you are an angry person. Can you get angry? Of course. You're human. All of us can. But you're an incredibly soft-spoken person.

Corey: I'm not a particularly angry person, but I felt like it was a denial thing. In a limited way they could support me, but when I really needed them I didn't get it. I was really raw. I was sort of a mess. Like I say often in my speeches, there is no road map. We don't teach in schools, usually, or in societies, what to do when you get sexually assaulted. We don't even have the basic conversations sometimes, let alone the more serious ones. We might have a preventative, "Here's what you do to be safe" conversation, but we don't have the conversation of, "If you get sexually assaulted here are the resources in your neighborhood. Here are some things you can do. Here are some choices."

My dad doesn't know what happened because the one time I tried to tell him he said that he didn't want to know. I just said, "Okay, Dad." After we hung up the phone, I was just like, "I wish I didn't know. In fact, I wish this didn't happen to me." I can understand him not wanting to know, but I don't have that privilege. Why am I supporting you in not knowing? How about you support me. How about that Dad…

I don't know if you want to talk about family, but I think it's important because the criminal justice system is so hard, and having the support of your family, or partners, or community can mean the difference in the healing process. My family unfortunately supported me not talking about it. I hate that. I hate that whole frame. I am so against that, because it's putting the burden back on me saying, "I'm going to tidy things up. I'm not going to talk about it. I'm not going to acknowledge and share with you what happened to me because you can't deal with it." Well I'm sorry. If you love me, and I am your family, I am your child. I am your child that is a survivor of sexual assault and that is part of it. And if you can't accept it, okay. But I am not going to be silent. I love them. I love them for who they are, but it's been ten and eleven years since both assaults, and being sexually assaulted still impacts my life.

Me: You talk about anger. You said you were angry for years. Was there a switch? Was there a defining moment when you said, "Now things are going to change"? If so, what was that? And what did you do about it?

Corey: The first thing that happened is I had my first serious relationship in 2006. That was pretty good. I think that helped. I've never been in a serious relationship with anybody. I had these two experiences of sexual assault. I had close relationships with men and dated them, but I wasn't sexually attracted to men. I really wanted to be, but I wasn't. I had my first relationship with a woman, and it wasn't just that I was emotionally and intellectually attracted to them, but I was also physically attracted and felt safe with this person that I dated. That was good. It showed me that I could be sexual, that I could be intimate and vulnerable with someone, and they weren't going to be terrible to me.

Basically at that point I had my walls up high. My ex helped with bringing those walls down, but it wasn't right away. It took her a little bit of time to get her chisel out and chip through. But the fact that we were able to establish a loving, caring, intimate relationship where I felt safe, comfortable, and loved was really good because it showed that I could trust people. I couldn't just trust anybody, but I could be vulnerable. I could tell my girlfriend very intimate parts of my life. I could really be open with her and trust her in a deeper way. I think that helped.

Me: What prompted you to become a THP survivor speaker? How did you hear about THP?

Corey: I learned more about THP when I heard Shira speak at the "Slut Walk", which is a march and protest against excusing rape by referring to any aspect of a woman's appearance, including the clothing that she wore during the assault. I knew a little bit about THP because I had done some activism work and met THP volunteers, but I hadn't heard a survivor speaker speak, and when I heard Shira speak…it was really powerful. I don't even remember exactly what she said, but I remember how I felt afterwards. I tried to find her and I think she was gone, but after that I looked it up.

It took me time because I was a little nervous, but I contacted THP and I got in touch with Carmen. Then last summer I did the training, which was intense, and we practiced writing down our story.

Corey wanted to take a break. After a few minutes we continued.

Corey: Something I want to talk about is filing charges. I feel really good about filing charges. When I look at the legal documents and know that he was found guilty even though his sentence was far from ideal, just having that validation that he was found guilty makes me feel good. But I really want to hit home the fact that for me, that was the right choice. But I think often that people try to police survivors' experiences and tell them how they should respond, and I do not wish to do that. I do not want my decisions to be generalized on other people. I won't say, "They should make that decision too," because it is a really hard decision to make. It's like experiencing a trauma and then being put through the ringer and being judged. Having to testify in a court of law is not a process that you want to do unless you have to.

In the first assault it was a decision I couldn't make even though I would have liked to. I just couldn't. Afterwards I did whole sweeps of my room to make sure he wasn't there. I felt so scared that because he knew where I went to school that he was going to come and attack me or stalk me. It's not an easy decision. We really do like to think of it as a just system and legal justice system, but I don't think it actually is a just system.
Me: It is for some.
Corey: Oh yeah.
Me: But it's not for all. And it may not be for most that experience sexual violence.
Corey: The system can be just. It's really the sexual violence that to me is the issue. I talk about my experience where I didn't feel like it was just. It definitely can be more just. I have hopes that in the last ten years it has become more just. I think and hope there is more awareness and sensitivity, but I did not experience it, unfortunately.

I find strength and hope in that I view survivors of sexual trauma as a community. People don't choose to be survivors of sexual violence, so this is not a community that would choose to be part of that community, but the root of my activism is identifying as a survivor of sexual trauma and being open about that.

One time this guy made a joke about molesting me. I was like, "ONE: You come near me and I'm kicking you in the shins, and TWO: That is not cool. That is not funny. That is not a joke."

I know our society loves to make jokes of things that it's uncomfortable with, but when you have been raped or sexually assaulted, it is not a joke. You are not going to say that around me without me saying something. Even if it's hard. Even if it's awkward. I will be the bad guy. I am not going to support someone normalizing rape and sexual assault. It is not okay, because that kind of behavior in some ways makes it more normal. You are not going to joke about rape and sexual assault around me. It's not visible that I am a survivor, but I feel comfortable in outing myself as a survivor when someone really crosses the line. I feel the need to let people know that stuff like that has a consequence. It has an effect. It's painful. It is PAINFUL to hear stuff like that.

This is not uplifting but it's important to me because I hear it a lot. When people don't know that I'm a survivor and they talk like that, it's just like, "You think it's funny, because to you I believe most often, rape is either sensationalized or this theoretical thing, but it maybe hasn't touched you, or maybe you are just compartmentalizing." It's like, "Rape, oh yeah, that's that thing that gets people all in arms so I'm going to use it to shock you." No, what you're doing is actually talking about something that AFFECTS a lot of people and acting like it's a joke, a novelty, a silly ha ha thing; it's not.

Rape, sexual assault, incest…these acts of sexual violence affects so many people. I just can't deal with people joking about them. It's not funny, and I can't support it. I know it's hard, but I challenge that kind of behavior. I don't do it in like an "Oh, you're bad" way. I do it like, "Hey, I'm not sure if you're aware, but when you joke about this it isn't okay. It just isn't. It's not cool, and here's why."

Sexual assault is not a theoretical thing. It is not some hypothetical conversation. It is something that happened to me twice in my life. It is something that has happened to people that I love and care about. It is not this thing that should be joked about like it's inconsequential because it isn't. It's so underreported.

I will use this word and I will own it. I think sexual assault is an epidemic. It is a crime that happens to a lot of people, but because of the shame around the sexual nature of the crime and because of how incredibly hard it is to come forward, that is why so many people do not come forward. The data is pretty high. Some say the numbers are one in four women and one in six men. But even these statistics, although shocking to those who don't know, are not completely accurate compared to how many cases of sexual assault are happening.

Me: I agree.

Corey: There are a lot of different factors. There is age, country of origin, language issues. Also, predators can be very good at putting fear into their victims. It's a problem when we don't have the conversation and we trivialize it. We talk about AIDS and other issues but...

Me: There are tons of issues, and all of the issues need to be talked about, but we're not really talking about rape. We're not really talking about sexual violence. It's fucked up.

Corey: The reason why I talk about it, the reason why I will stand out in front of a crowd of people and say, "I was sexually assaulted and I am not ashamed," is because we don't fucking talk about it. That perpetuates this environment where people who are sexually assaulted struggle. I really struggled. I had a really hard time and I didn't have the support I needed. I have more support now, and that has been part of my healing process.

Me: You say sexual violence is an epidemic. I completely agree with you. What do we do about that epidemic? It's difficult to reduce and difficult to stop.

Corey: I support the notion, but before we can even think about stopping sexual violence we need to really get real and honest and have these conversations. I feel like most often sexual assault is reduced to dramatic interpretations. The stories usually have very black and white, very victimizing, very disempowering story lines. It is not survivors telling their own story; it's dramatized in the media, and that is sometimes where people get their information. That is not the worst thing ever, but it is not a survivor telling their own personal story and talking about their experience. It is a dramatic interpretation. It is a story produced for entertainment. I don't watch stories or movies about rape. To me, sexual violence is not entertainment.

Me: You say it is an epidemic. To me, you help the epidemic by speaking. By talking. By getting out there in the public. By letting people know it is real and that it happens to a lot of people. By letting people know they are not alone. And then things start to change. In my own experiences as a THP counselor, from what I've seen, things start to change when people start to speak. I was at the rally with you. I saw the looks on the people's faces. When you spoke, did you feel in that moment you were empowering other people for them to go out and speak for themselves?

Corey: Mostly people thanked me for speaking. And what I said to them was, "Thank you for being here and expressing a commitment to challenging rape culture." The whole point of me speaking is that I want the people to ask the questions. Even though sometimes the hard questions are really hard, I want to open up the dialogue. I try in my speeches to be the most human and open. I usually try to be funny because I want to show people that I am a survivor, I wear that hat, I fly that flag around, but I'm also just a person. And to me, I do think I helped create change even though it's hard for me to admit that.

I notice a relative lack of honest conversations about sexual assault, or the conversations stop, or they never happen. I want them to happen. I want people to feel like they can talk about it, because when we don't, I think it perpetuates sexual assault. It is disempower-

ing survivors when we don't talk about it. I want to, in my own way, support survivors because while I don't know what individual people went through, I know what I went through, and I can at least sort of understand and want to be a part of a positive change.

It's really hard for some people when I say I'm a trauma survivor. They don't know what to say or what to do. Sometimes they just don't want to say the wrong thing, and I say to them, "It is okay. I may not know the answer, but there isn't a wrong question. Just ask me the question." Because we do not talk about this stuff enough. We do not. I would rather be vulnerable with you in that space and answer the questions and talk about things that are painful and be a real human being because I don't want the conversation to just be plot lines. They are just stories. But I am not a story. I am a real, normal, relatively average, flawed human being. Just like most other people.

Me: Just like everyone. We are all flawed.

Corey: To other survivors: Know that things do get better. For me they have, but it's not like some amount of time goes by and erases what happened. While I have been able to do some things to transform, it is still hard. I want people to see those scars a little bit. I don't want to push them in people's faces and make the conversation more difficult, but I do want to show the effect. I want it to be personal and have people understand the effect. When there is a face and it becomes more personal, there is more understanding of the effects.

Someone once asked me if sexual assault made me gay. People have asked about my family. Someone once asked me if I ever lived with roommates again. The conversation we're having is valuable. That is my activism, and that is where my heart is. To me, there's pretty much nothing more important that I do than having these conversations because each conversation is speaking against that silence and that shame. Us not talking about it is part of the problem, and I will not be part of the problem when it comes to sexual violence.

I know how it feels. It is my story. I am Corey, and I am a survivor. It is my story. It is my story twice. Twice. I was sexually assaulted while doing a sexual assault internship. That is hard to say. That is hard to talk about. But every opportunity I have to speak through THP, I will go out and tell it. It helps me. It helps me to own it. I'd rather tell my story in my own words than someone else tell my story. As painful as it is to be vulnerable in that way, being able to say it in my way, in my own words and know that it is my personal story is empowering. It empowers me. It's not some monologue that I'm reading. It's everything that I've lived through. And just because it's painful and was a low point in my life, it isn't now. Hell, I can stand up and speak in front of two hundred people. Ten years ago? No. It was something that was brutally horrible in my life. But now? I am strong. I am fucking strong.

So often the narratives are, "You're a victim." No! I am strong. You can try to put whatever words you want on me. I do not care. I will not accept that. I am not a victim. There are some days when I don't always feel totally like a survivor, but at least the word "survivor" is empowering. I went through these terrible, traumatic experiences, and I've come through it. I don't believe I will ever completely heal, but I can be strong. I can be vulnerable, and I can also challenge a lot of assumptions and victim blaming behavior. One time during a speech someone asked, "Is there anything you could have done differently to avoid what happened?" I said, "I did the best I could, but there isn't an answer there. You want me to tell you what I could have done. And there isn't an answer there. There is not an answer because it isn't what I did."

Bobby, you are the choir. Most of those people at the rally are the choir. I don't need to reach them as much as I need to reach the person that is trying to blame me for being sexually assaulted. People that are already active and doing the work get it. But I do also need to reach people that don't think about it, that aren't engaged, and that don't get it.

Me: Is there one final message you want people to take away?

Corey: For me, the main goal I have in doing this kind of activism and talking to you is letting people know that incidences of sexual assault are way more common than anyone would think. I think that is really important…focus on that… focus on the fact that this particular crime is happening to so many people. I have talked to so many people and I've heard their stories. I have listened to them tell me their story. I've heard so many stories, and every story I hear just adds to the main fact, which to me, is that it is so prevalent. Forget statistics. Almost every time I disclose that I am a survivor, several people disclose to me. It's hard to hear someone's story, or just hear that they are a survivor, because to me it's indicative of how vast the problem is, and how much we really need to start talking about it and have the hard conversations.

There are a lot of barriers to progress, but there are also not. What I do isn't that sensational. To me, it's just a matter of taking that risk and being vulnerable and not being ashamed to say, "I'm a survivor." I have transformed what that means to me and have come this far. Yes, I have a trauma history, but I am in a completely different place now. I draw power in that. I felt so good after my speech on Saturday. I felt really proud of myself. I heard the people roar. I do this kind of activism because I believe in it whole-heartedly, and it allows me to use what happened to me as tool to speak out against sexual violence.

Chapter 10

JUSTICE

———

"The most important thing is that there absolutely are options there. There are a lot of different legal options that people might not know about, so it's great to talk to someone who can help them figure that out. But there is no right or wrong decision. There really isn't. It really is individual."

What is justice? Is it just that Corey's perpetrator received two years probation and a fine of $250 for sexual assault? Is it just that some drug offenders spend more time in prison than sex offenders? Is it just that most rapists are not even arrested let alone incarcerated? I could not tell you how many rape disclosures I have received throughout my life, but I have received at least fifty. Of all the disclosures I've listened to and all the stories I know, there is only one person I know of who has been incarcerated for rape or sexual assault. How is that just? What does justice look like to those who have been sexually violated, but never seen their perpetrator or perpetrators punished in any way?

A friend of mine once asked me, "Hey Bobby, how is social injustice treating you?" This book is not about the criminal justice system, but I believe it is imperative to at least write about justice, or lack there of. None of the survivors sharing their stories in this book have seen their perpetrators incarcerated. What does justice look like to them and anyone else who has these experiences?

Megan never saw her perpetrator incarcerated. She wrote a poem that she would like to share with you called, *"And She Refuses Justice"*.

And She Refuses Justice
(I wrote this in response to someone asking what I would do if my detective came back to me and offered me a chance to put my molester in jail - a fate that did not await him when I was sixteen)

Officer, you come to me
To tell me I've a chance
To show the world how right I am
And how wrong the Other was.
But what does that accomplish?
I ask you straight forward and plain.
What possible good will that do for me?
What restitution will that serve for agonies past?
So he finally gets what he deserves and I am left with
What?
A half decade's revenge satisfied?
The momentary bliss of knowing I was right?
Will it change the minds of those who still believe it was
All My Fault?
No. It won't. Because nothing shifts a tumor.
Nothing moves a dead tree that doesn't want to die.
Their minds were made up before the last word of the story
Fell upon their broken ears.
Long ago I made peace with the fact that I am not always
To be right.

To be righted.
You want to give me justice for the pain and the anguish I suffered?
Take from me my agonies.
This smoldering coal lump in my soul
And plant them deep inside of him
So he can never be whole.
Aside from that, oh mortal avenger,
There's nothing you can do.
Please feel not the strain of obligation
For a girl who won't say yes.
The world is so much brighter, clearer
Than it was before.
I don't struggle as my peers have done
for who I'm supposed to be.
I suppose
Spending so much time as someone else
From this, I learned to be free.
So, please take your vengeful offer
And file it away. Because, I'm sorry, Officer
There won't be justice today.

For Tim - (my investigator)

Blurry days with no sun
Moving through the motions
Marionetted and disjointed.
Unwilling to remember the slightest detail.
Unable to recall papered trysts
And promises.
Suddenly a hand grabs me by the collar
Yanks me from my darkened revelry

And demands a flood of memories.
Did he do it or did he not?
Explain further and in detail.
Please leave nothing out.
Clarity astounded me as I looked into Hand's face
And gave him what he needed.
Did exactly what he asked.
No matter fear weakened my knees
And shook my voice in sorrow.
Picked up a phone, continued on
Kept waking to tomorrow.
And why? What pulled me from my daze?
What forced me to see daylight?
A single hand reached out in aid.
A stranger sent to free me
Who soldiered on long after
To pull others from their darkness.
A gift from God? A job well done? Well, who will ever know?
But one small girl torn from the wash
And forced up to the sun.

Working with Joan as a case management intern was great, but I found it just as helpful and fulfilling to work with Aila, the head of the Legal Department at THP. Aila is a compassionate, caring, sweet, empathetic, and brilliant woman. She is another special human being that is rare to find, but I'm thankful I did.

I loved helping Aila out with the legal cases and enjoyed learning about the legal system. She, like Joan, taught me how to be a better counselor and person. I admired her for the work she did, but also for the work she didn't do. Aila can do anything in the world she wants. She could easily be rich by being a prominent lawyer at a well known law firm, but she chooses to make a lot less money by working at THP as a legal advocate for rape survivors.

Aila was more than willing to sit down with me and have a conversation for this book. I wanted her to explain the legal options survivors have and to help sort out the question of justice. She is the expert, not me. I organized this so that she is talking directly to you. I want you to know what she and her department do and to fully understand many of the options survivors and significant others have. I hope this helps if you have been affected by sexual violence and feel that you have not received your form of justice. Justice is different for everyone, and Aila can best explain what that means and what options people have going forward. This was our conversation:

Me: So what exactly do you do? What has your experience been like working at THP?

Aila: We try to make sure that survivors understand all of their options. We try to help them understand the benefits, and the possibly negative, or just consequences in general of accessing those options. And thinking through what it would mean for someone tomorrow, six months from now, two years from now in terms of what their participation is going to need to be, or how it's going to affect their lives or the lives of the people around them. So our main focus is to make sure survivors understand all of their options, criminal and civil legal options. We also make sure that they understand timeframes too, so that they understand that this may only be an option for them within a certain amount of time, and they don't have to take that option, but if they don't do that option now, it's not going to be available to them later. That really is an important thing that we do.

Depending on what a survivor wants and what their version or description of justice is, we will help them figure out how to get there if it's possible. Even for the legal issues, we work through the empowerment model and just accept that regardless of our personal thoughts around it, or whether we're concerned a survivor may want this option vs. another option, as long as ethically we feel like we can help them access it we will. That's the main thing that we do.

We will talk to some survivors for half an hour over the phone and that's it. They just want some information and then maybe they move forward with it or maybe they don't. Others want us to be there for them to check in with, but they want to do everything on their own. And then others really want us to be the main person helping them get there and just be there with them every step of the way. So our involvement is as little or as much as they want us to be there.

Me: In terms of percentages, do a lot of survivors who request THP's services go forward with the legal process? Or do most not? Is it hard to gauge?

Aila: My guess would probably be 50/50. And it might be that they are moving forward on one thing and not other things.

Me: What do you mean by that?

Aila: I think a lot of survivors do come to us because they want to know about the criminal justice system and reporting to the police, but it doesn't necessarily mean that they would move forward with that. But as we're talking to them, we may be able to help identify other issues that they haven't necessarily thought of as legal. This can mean in terms of their rights as an employee or their rights as a student. We may be talking to them about everything and they may decide, "Reporting to the police isn't for me but I really want to feel safe on my campus until I graduate, so reporting to my university is the way that I want to go." So I'll go with that option even though it wasn't something they were really thinking about when they called us.

Me: So we're not just talking about criminal or civil court?

Aila: Right. There are a lot of negotiations.

Me: Do you mind explaining what that means?

Aila: When we talk about civil legal issues, it may be that someone is filing a civil lawsuit against a third party or the perpetrator. And for those issues we would send them to a private civil attorney, and there are some really great ones that really focus on sexual assault issues and moving forward with those cases. But for a lot of survivors it's much more about, "I need to take three weeks off of work and

I want to know how much I have to tell my employer under our human resources policy so that I can take that time without putting everything out there about what I'm going through", or "I just want to know what my rights are. How much time can I take off? Will they penalize me? Will it be used against me?"

Talking to them about those things that they can do is very important. They may not necessarily be in the legal system, but there are legal rights and obligations out there in terms of employers and universities and what they need to do. Maybe they're just having some financial concerns, so we can help them figure out what they can do around that, like applying for victim's compensation through the state, or finding other avenues available to them. A little bit of case management comes into that. They might need to apply for short-term or long-term disability. For housing, much of it is doing a housing search, but it may also be thinking about if they're in a private landlord/tenant situation; how do you break that lease? What are their obligations as a tenant? What are the landlord's obligations to them? So things like that.

And of course safety always comes up. They can apply for a restraining order and not do anything else. They don't have to report to the police. They don't have to report to anyone else to try and get a restraining order.

Me: Do the survivors talk about their perpetrators? Are they still present in their lives? Or do they not talk about that?

Aila: It depends on the situation. A lot of times we can help people figure out their options without knowing any details. We might need to know a little bit just in terms of whom the perpetrator is and the kind of contact they have on a regular basis, and what the perpetrator knows about them so that we can assess their safety options. We can figure things out such as, "Okay, if you tell your employer what happens, what is that going to mean to you in terms of safety because you work with the perpetrator?" Sometimes it's the perpetrator's best friend. So we may need to know a little bit, but often we don't get into details at all. There are some clients that I've worked with for years that I don't know the specifics at all about what happened to them. I just know generally who the perpetrator is and how we need to work around that to keep them safe and to maintain their privacy.

Me: In my opinion based on my experiences, a lot of people know about rape and think, "You have to go to court. You have to get a conviction. That person has to be incarcerated." I do not think that is what is going on in terms of percentages. Is that fair to say?

Aila: Oh that's absolutely true.

Me: Why is that?

Aila: The criminal justice system isn't really set up for sexual assault cases to respond well and appropriately. I think for some survivors it works really well, but for a lot of survivors, particularly when it's a non-stranger sexual assault, the dynamics that come into that don't play well for what the prosecutors need to move forward with the case. There's not a lot of evidence usually. There aren't things like a lot of physical injury. There aren't witnesses usually. The relationship that the perpetrator and the survivor may have had before the assault may have been friendly. There may have been some consensual sexual contact. So those are all things that make it very difficult for a prosecutor to look at and say, "I feel like I can move forward with this case and possibly meet the burden of proof and see this person convicted." For most cases that we see, they don't go forward.

Me: Is it mainly because of the lack of evidence?

Aila: I think that's part of it. I think that prosecutors feel like these cases are difficult to prove because often there isn't any evidence.

Me: So do some survivors really want to go forward, but then the prosecutor looks at all of the information and says, "We can't do it"?

Aila: Yeah. I would say anecdotally, the majority of people who do decide to report to the police, the concern ultimately ends up being that their case isn't going to go forward and the survivor wants the case to go forward. And it's not their decision to make because once you report you become a witness in the state's case against the perpetrator. So it ultimately is up to the District Attorney's office whether they are going to go forward or not. They will listen to what the survivor wants, but if they feel like they can't move forward with the evidence then they won't. And that's why these other avenues are so important for survivors to know about, so they can get some form of justice.

Me: In your experience and your opinion, why do you think people do not report to the police?

Aila: They are afraid that they will not be believed. They have this idea of what a victim should look like from the media.

Me: Which is what?

Aila: I think a lot of people think, "I don't look like someone who has been assaulted. I don't have any injuries. It wasn't a stranger. I'm not even sure if what happened to me is a crime. Even though I feel like it's a violation, I'm not sure if legally it actually is rape because I knew this person, because I consented to some things, or I spent time with them voluntarily. I trusted them." That comes up a lot. They are often worried about what people are going to think about their decisions before and after an assault. Maybe someone didn't tell anyone for a long time or didn't go to the hospital right away, or wasn't able to label it for themselves as rape for a long time. So those things will come up. Sometimes they are worried about the perpetrator. They're worried that maybe the perpetrator will retaliate, or they're in a community where they're worried that other people will retaliate because they've put this out there about the perpetrator.

Me: So not only is there a fear of not being believed, there is also a fear of potentially more victimization? More violence? More extreme violence?

Aila: Absolutely. Or just rumors being started, or people blaming the survivors and not the perpetrators. So if the perpetrator is in this tight community, probably other people look at this person as a good person and wouldn't understand what happened. But sometimes too, they're feeling like, "I don't want the perpetrator in trouble." If there are some immigration issues going on, they might be worried that the perpetrator might be deported. They might depend on the perpetrator economically. The perpetrator might be a family member who the whole family depends on emotionally. Or just in general, they might feel like, "That's just not my version of justice. My version of justice is I want to move on with my life and just feel safe, but I don't want to see the perpetrator go to jail." I think there are a lot of different reasons why people decide not to report.

Me: What is justice?

Aila: That's the…

Me: Seriously. What is your…

Aila: I can't…I think just being able to move forward in a way that feels safe and healthy. And I don't think for a lot of people going through the criminal justice system will give them justice.

Me: Which is ironic given that the criminal justice system is supposed to entail justice and our safety.

Aila: And for some people it does and it will. But I really feel like you can't define it. Only the survivor can define it. For some survivors, it's really as basic as "I want to change my locks. If I can just get my landlord to agree to let me change my locks, I'll feel safe in my apartment and that's all I want from you. That's all I need to move forward." Or it might just be, "I want to change my shifts at work so I don't have to see this person anymore, and as long as I don't have to see them, that's it. I don't need anything else." And for others, it definitely entails a lot more in terms of, "I want to move out of the community", or "I want to get a new job", or "I want that person off campus while I'm continuing to go to school." So it can mean a lot of different things, but it doesn't always mean, "I want this person to be convicted or found responsible in a public way for what happened."

Me: I've always been interested in the psychological impact of crime, but specifically this crime since I've volunteered at THP. My opinion is that many people don't dig deep enough to understand the impacts. I think plenty of people just think about crime, arrest, court, incarceration or no incarceration, end of story. I don't believe we fully understand the psychological effects people have from rape. I say this because of my experiences interacting with survivors, but specifically something that happened with a client I worked with at THP. This woman was so adamant about taking her perpetrator to court. I said, "That's great. We support you." And then a week later she called me and said, "I can't do it." I said, "That's okay. You have time. We're still here if you ever want to go forward in the future." What do you think happened? What changed for her? And what does that look like for the others just like her?

Aila: It might be a few different things. I think one thing is that going through the system can be really tough. There are a lot of great detectives. There are a lot of great District Attorneys out there that really do their job well and they care about the survivors they work with. But it's a difficult process, even if you have the best support in place. It's a long process. It takes a year to two years if it even got to trial. So it takes a toll on a survivor. They have to talk to a detective, an Assistant District Attorney, and have to provide explicit details. At some point they will have to testify before a grand jury, and then at some point they will have to testify in an open courtroom. So those things can all feel overwhelming and difficult, especially if you're on this track where you're trying to heal and it keeps being brought up in a way that doesn't feel healthy for that person. So that can be one thing.

The other thing could be that someone is reporting or thinking that they need to report because that is what you're supposed to do if you're a victim. And that's what everyone thinks you're supposed to do if you're a victim. There is a mentality of, "Of course you should report it to the police if this really happened to you." But it's not something that they feel personally they want to do or are ready for. I think sometimes people do it because they think they should. They think they need to protect other possible victims or they think they need to do it because everyone around them is saying, "This is what you have to do next."

But sometimes if they're able to take a step back and realize that that's really not what they want to do. It's not something they feel comfortable with. And hopefully they come to the realization that as hard as it is, that it's not their responsibility to prevent this from happening to anyone else. The responsibility is only on the perpetrator. So they might get to that place where they feel comfortable with that decision and realize that, "I don't want to do this." But the other piece could be that they may have had a negative interaction, or what they perceive to be a negative interaction with someone who is part of the system and it just made them realize that "This is going to be too much for me. It's not worth it."

Me: I've been fascinated by the disparity of our sentencing. I once sat in prison with inmates for class while I was in college. All of us sat in a circle and talked. Only two inmates admitted what they did. One guy received six years and another guy received nine years for selling drugs. The other inmates would not say what they did, but I later learned that they were convicted sex offenders. Some received two and four years. I thought to myself, *Something is seriously wrong with this. Something seems off.*

Aila: I agree.

Me: That was mind blowing to me, but as we've already discussed, if the DA even brings the case to trial.

Aila: Yeah, which for most cases you don't really see that many. There's a better chance it's going to go forward if it's a stranger assault.

Me: Given that most cases don't even get to trial, what is the next best thing for a survivor? I ask because the crimes still exist. The effects still exist. What is the next best option for them? We talked about justice for themselves, assuming they attain it. What else is the next best thing for them given that they may not get to a certain point in the criminal justice system?

Aila: I do think it's figuring what they, WHAT THEY, and only them, what they really want and need. And just making sure that there are agencies out there, people out there that can help them get to that, so that they can just live their best life, so that they can integrate this and heal and move on and get whatever they feel is justice for them. A lot of times it really is true: Justice can just mean being able to move past this in a way that they can continue to live a life they want to live, and not having this derail them in a way that is so detrimental to them in their lives because they didn't have the support that they may have needed to move on.

I think for most survivors that we work with, that really is the best thing for them. And it often isn't about a concrete, "This person was found guilty", or "This person was found responsible", or whatever it might be. It definitely is more than that. It can be, "I was able to stay in school and graduate and I'm in the career I always wanted to be in and that didn't derail me", or "I'm able to continue the relationships I have that were starting to fall apart afterwards because I wasn't getting the counseling that I needed." Whatever it might be.

Me: Is there anything that you specifically want to tell people about this issue? This crime? Is there anything else that you want to add?

Aila: The most important thing is that there absolutely are options there. There are a lot of different legal options that people might not know about, so it's great to talk to someone who can help them figure that out. But there is no right or wrong decision. There really isn't. It really is individual.

There are a lot of different things that people can decide to do that will work for them and be the best thing for them. No one should feel like they have to do something after an assault because they don't. They don't have to do anything they don't want to do or don't feel comfortable with. They don't have to participate in the criminal justice system that they may feel like is not going to be the best thing for them because they think it's their duty or they think they should. I think that's the most important thing, just so they know that there's just no right part when it comes to legal issues. It really depends on what they want.

Chapter 11

VICTIM BLAMING

—

"All I know is that believing I was to blame was easier for them than accepting that this person they all revered was a pedophile. It was easier to blame a child."

I have worked with clients on case management and legal issues, facilitated educational workshops at colleges and universities, and tabled health events in poor and rich communities, yet no matter where I go, I still hear victim blaming statements. Why are some survivors blamed for being raped and sexually assaulted? It sickens me every time I hear it, and I think it is worth thinking about and discussing. Some people wonder why survivors don't *get over it*. Part of the reason why some survivors don't *get over it* is because they have been blamed, as if they somehow are responsible for being raped or sexually assaulted. Victim blaming will often make a survivor feel even worse, which may make the healing process that much harder.

I believe it is illogical, disgusting, and slightly insane to blame someone who has been raped or sexually assaulted for being raped or sexually assaulted. I'm not sure if those who blame understand the impact of that blame on someone else, but the effects are very damaging. Victim blaming is arguably the biggest deterrent to one's growth and healing, and yet as simple as it is, believing and listening to someone can often times be the most important things survivors need when they disclose. If we believe, listen, and validate, we strengthen and help. If we blame, we confuse and hurt.

I once spoke to a college class of ten women. I asked the class if they blame women who are raped if they are under the influence of alcohol at the time of the rape. Fifty percent of the women raised their hands. I asked one student if she had ever drunk alcohol in her life. She laughed and said, "I'm Irish." I laughed and said, "I'm part Irish too. What do you like to drink? I love beer, Italian red wine and vodka." I then said, "Imagine the next time you go out drinking and your friend rapes you. Imagine you found the courage to tell someone, and the first thing they said to you was, 'Why were you drinking?' How do you think that would make you feel? Do you think that would make you feel horrible?" I told her she blamed complete strangers for the exact same thing she did quite often. The only difference between her and the strangers she blamed is she didn't get raped. She pondered my questions and statements and seemed to understand what I was trying to convey. I hope she did anyways.

Another woman in the class wanted to challenge me because she described herself as a non-drinker. I asked her if she had ever had a glass of wine in her life. She said she had. I then said, "Imagine you fall in love with a man. Imagine that you really believe in your heart that you have met the man you are going to marry. Now imagine that this man takes you on a romantic dinner. During dinner you have a glass of wine to compliment the delicious meal, as wine often does. Think about how beautiful the night is going and how much you love this man. Now imagine you go home after dinner and he rapes you. How horrible would you feel if we blamed you for having a glass of wine during dinner? Are you not allowed to have a glass of wine at dinner with the man you love?"

I then asked, "What if you didn't have a glass of wine at all and he still raped you? What if you drank water? What is the difference?" I then explained to the whole class that it doesn't matter if alcohol is involved or not. No one should be blamed for being raped while intoxicated. I then explained that some people are raped when they are completely sober. Drunk or sober, they are not to blame. They are never to blame.

A woman once disclosed to me that she wanted to take her rapist to court but was told by friends not to. They questioned her because she was drunk while it happened. They said she would ruin his life. They argued he was so smart and had so much going for him in terms of school and his career. They said he would be extremely successful and that a conviction would ruin his life. I told this woman that he had ruined his own life by raping a woman, assuming he even received a conviction.

I once met a man who thought a woman deserved to get raped if her thong hung out of her pants. I told this man that some women are raped whether they have a thong hanging out or not. I told him it doesn't matter if a woman is dressed provocatively or not. No woman deserves to get raped. I then proceeded to say that men and little boys are also raped. He did not grasp the fact that male rape exists. I tried my best to explain to him that some men and boys are raped, regardless of the clothes they are wearing or not wearing, or regardless of any kind of clothing or underwear that might be hanging out. He was disgusted by the thought that a man could be raped, but didn't seem to be disgusted by the fact that women are raped.

Other people blame survivors for hanging out with a rapist. They will say things like, "How could you hang out with him! What the hell is wrong with you!" These people don't seem to understand that the lunatic hiding in the bushes or under bridges accounts for a minority of rapes and sexual assaults. They don't seem to understand that most rapists are viewed as nice people. Rapists exist within every gender, ethnicity, religion, job profession, socio-economic status, and sexual orientation. Is a person not supposed to go on a date? Is a person not supposed to be with his or her spouse? Is an altar server not supposed to be around a priest? Is a child not supposed to hang out with relatives?

These are just some of the victim blaming statements I have heard in my life. I believe people should contemplate the fact that some survivors unfortunately have to hear and see it themselves. I believe people need to understand that victim blaming statements hurt survivors. Victim blaming statements can make a survivor feel bad about him or herself. They can make a survivor not want to open up and speak. They can make a survivor actually believe he or she is to blame for what happened to them, which isn't true because the survivor is not to blame. Victim blaming ultimately leads to more confusion, pain, and problems as opposed to clarity, healing, and growth.

This is the victim blaming that Megan experienced:

Megan: In the immediate aftermath of Mike being arrested and the prosecution going forward, I ran into his wife in a local shopping center. I hadn't seen her since everything had happened and I was desperate for comfort. In order to understand what happens next, you need to understand that Mike and Nikki (his then-wife) were like aunt and uncle to me. The two of them simultaneously molded my voice and encouraged my dreams of vocal stardom while contributing to my growth as a young adult. Nikki meant the world to me, so when I saw her coming out of a local Mexican restaurant while my mom and I were grocery shopping, I couldn't help myself. I leapt out of the backseat of the minivan and sprinted towards her.

"Nikki! Hi!" I said breathlessly.

"Hi, Megan." She was reserved and I found very quickly that this was not going to go in my favor.

"Um, how are you?" I was desperate. This woman who had once cared so much for me was looking at me with disdain.

"I'm fine, Megan. I can't talk to you right now. I need to go."

I have never had a more icy reception in my life. I walked with marked confusion back to my mother's car and closed the door behind me.

"What happened?" she asked.

"I have no idea," I managed before the tears began to flow.

A few days later we heard that Nikki and many of her close friends in our vocal studio were maintaining the belief that not only was the molestation my fault, but it was also my fault that their marriage was failing. I didn't understand the logic then and I don't understand it now. All I know is that believing I was to blame was easier for them than accepting that this person they all revered was a pedophile. It was easier to blame a child.

If you have been raped or sexually assaulted and you have been blamed, or fear that you may be blamed, I just want you to understand this: You are not to blame. There is nothing you did to make someone hurt you, nor is there anything you could have done differently to prevent or stop it. If we are to blame anyone, we should blame a person who chooses to rape.

Chapter 12

MEGAN

———

"I have dreams. I dream like everyone else dreams. Fall into that REM cycle and off to la-la land I go. But I have nightmares. I have nightmares that I don't think other people have. All of my nightmares center on the same topic: not being able to scream loud enough to be heard. The most frightening thing I dream is that he has kidnapped me.

Now, let me say before I go on that he is not, in real life, nearly as frightening, menacing, and all-powerful as he is in my mind while I sleep. He's just a guy. A guy I was in love with once. A guy who made a choice one night not to listen to me. To have selective hearing. To only hear me when I said yes. To ignore the 300 'no's' that preceded it. But, still, he's just a guy.

In my dreams, though, he is the all-powerful, terrifying lord of my life. He takes me, I presume, at some point in the dream that I never remember. But I remember rolling over in my dream-bed and seeing him there, staring at me. And I try to back away. I try to gracefully exit the situation without angering the monster beside me. I never succeed. I get out the door and he drags me back in by my ankles. I scream. I scream as loud as I possibly can in a dream. But he just laughs. He sits there with my ankles in his hands and laughs.

He rolls me on my stomach on the floor of this apartment I now recognize as his domain. He sticks it in me and he pounds on my back while he pushes in and out of me. And I cry. And I try to scream again. And he laughs. And no one hears me. No one cares to hear me. Just like that night in real life. I cried and I sobbed, but no one heard me. Correction: No one chose to hear me. And I don't know why."

I value the survivors and their stories so much, and ultimately believe their words are the best way to connect to other human beings. I believe their stories are extremely meaningful and beneficial for others, so I wanted to compile as many as possible. I asked my boss to send an email to the THP survivor speakers to see if they wanted to contribute to this book. I couldn't have been more ecstatic with the response by the group. I received four emails in one day from survivors who wanted to share their stories. One of the survivors who responded is Megan.

Megan and I exchanged a few emails and then met for the first time to grab a coffee. Megan had an intense excitement as she listened to my ideas about this book. I quickly learned that Megan is a very pleasant person to be around. She is thoughtful, caring, and passionate. She has an uncanny ability to make you feel comfortable instantly. She kindly gave me encouraging words throughout our discussion. I walked away from our interaction inspired.

Megan lifted my spirits and offered to help in any way. Her joy and enthusiasm made me happy. She was good to me and she encouraged me. Encouragement really does go a long way with people. I have been very insecure about this book at many different stages of the writing process, but she helped me get the insecurities out of my head by encouraging and strengthening me with her words and passion for helping other survivors.

It amazes me how Megan can somehow look and sound extremely comfortable while telling her story. I first listened to Megan share her story to about twenty-five college students. After she spoke, I watched her answer any questions the students had for her. She actually welcomed questions in hopes of helping the students. Her calmness and ability to answer anything is impressive. Megan looked more comfortable telling people about her experiences with sexual violence than I did talking about basketball during a public speaking course while I was in college.

The survivor speaker engagement then turned into an open forum discussion. The students asked Megan many questions, and occasionally I would chime in to make a relevant point when I thought it needed to be made. I can't remember how it came up, but I told the students that many survivors believe they will die during a rape. I looked at Megan as a survivor, but she did not see herself as a survivor. She told everyone that she does not identify herself as a survivor. Hearing her say that fascinated me because I learned even more about how people identify or don't identify themselves in regards to sexual violence. I asked Megan to elaborate if she thought it was relevant for the purposes of this book. She did, and this is what she wants to share with you:

Megan: When I was fifteen, my voice teacher of five and a half years (then forty-seven) spent a year attempting to convince me to screw him – in the process committing what amounted to a misdemeanor in California (don't get me started). You'd think that one brush with sexual assault would be enough for a lifetime, but when I was twenty I began dating a boy who made sex my duty and then one night flatly refused to take no for an answer and raped me. Still, I don't call myself a survivor.

Five years ago if you had asked me why I don't use that label, I would have told you that what had happened to me wasn't "enough" for me to count myself among the ranks of women who have had, surely, much worse things happen to them. What did I do, really? So I singlehandedly managed to hold off a forty-seven year old man bent on fucking me, and only "allowed" him to kiss me, fondle me, call me his girlfriend, and take over my life. The DA himself told me that it wasn't enough to accuse him of his intended crime. Is that survival? Well, perhaps it is, but it isn't enough to count myself as one of those strong, unwavering women I see in my work.

Shortly after my own introduction to THP, I realized that these things were "enough" and began to count myself a survivor as well. But then I was raped by someone I trusted; a rape I didn't even realize classified as such until a year later. I thought about all I had done since that day in July and asked myself if that could be counted as survival. In the most basic sense of the word, I suppose you could consider pulling away from everything before throwing myself into my work and school, finding a new, wonderful man and making a relationship with him, and happily moving on to be survival. But I? I just considered it living. I was living. Continuously living through whatever life threw at me. So, no, I don't call myself a survivor; I call myself a successful human being.

Fifteen months later...

Megan: When you asked me to write something about why I haven't referred to myself as a "survivor", I gave you, essentially, this: "I don't feel like what happened to me is enough. I feel like calling myself a survivor is a debasement of the experiences I hear from the people I work with on a daily basis." And then, as I was re-reading what I had given you and synopsizing it in my head, I realized that the synopsis, the basis of what I had written for you, did not actually include my words. The words I gave you were his, and that sort of knocked me on my ass because I had never realized how much I had internalized that.

The day after Tommy raped me, he came to my dorm to visit. I kicked my roommates out, sat him down, and told him that I felt he had used me (I couldn't bring myself to say the word rape because I was still under the impression that he loved me and I didn't believe that someone who loved me could rape me). I remember his reaction vividly: He sat back on my little dresser, looked straight at me and said, "Saying that to me is a disgrace to all the real survivors you work with on a daily basis." I didn't know what to say to that. I don't even remember what I did end up saying, but that phrase burned itself into my memory and seems to have wormed its way into my own self-concept: That calling myself a survivor somehow makes light of all the "real survivors" I work with. And I hadn't really ever identified with being a survivor because of that until I started working where I work now as a Victim Advocate.

Now, I realize the power of being able to say to someone in my office, "I understand you. I've been where you are. I'm a survivor too." I realized as I read what I had given you that I had come into calling myself a survivor because of all the other people I work with. I reframed my self-concept because of them. I call myself a survivor now. I identify with it. I know that what happened to me is enough and I am trying very hard to let go of what he said to me, to let it out of my self-concept, and make way for that word, that powerful, life-changing word: survivor.

I have only known Megan for a short amount of time, but I am thankful our paths have crossed. She has been very supportive and has helped push me to keep writing. Megan does everything in her power to help, support, empower, and teach people. She would like you to know that you can persevere through any effects caused by sexual violence. Physical, mental, emotional, and spiritual growth is very real and possible, evidenced by Megan and so many others. This is Megan's story:

One Year Later

A month ago, as I sat on the train riding home from work, I began to wonder: When did it happen? I know that it was summer & that it was hot because I was unbearable sticky, and even if I had not just been raped and told to shut up my crying, I would not have been able to sleep. I scoured my Facebook for clues, my journal, my blog, anything that would tell me when this had happened. I couldn't find it. I had so diligently erased him from my life all those months ago. I didn't know why it had suddenly become so important to me, but I needed to know. I needed a date to pin it down, to keep it in one place, pinned mercilessly to a calendar and left there to whither.

And then, as I was following my brain down the at times dark and at times cruelly bright memories of my time with him, I remembered: I had tried to write that night. Trying to talk to him hadn't worked. Trying to leave the room for a moment to call my mom got me only a threat to leave me alone in the bed while he went upstairs to sleep. So instead, I fell into a fitful sleep until I knew that he was unconscious, woke, and typed on my iPod. I scrambled for the little device, now cracked from a drop almost a year ago (a fitting aesthetic touch if I do say so myself) and clicked into the Notes app I hadn't opened in forever. There it was, sitting there benignly waiting to be remembered:

July 5, 2010

I feel…God, I feel awful, like the world has imploded in my stomach, like I've sacrificed a piece of myself for a few moments of someone else's peace.
I feel…used. I feel used because I didn't want it. He wanted it. So I automatically felt like I had to want it because if I didn't that makes me a bad girlfriend.
I feel like I'm going to throw up. I just spent four hours sleeping through nightmares of him leaving me.

I cried then. I let it come. I let myself cry for the self that had written this terrified, alone, sick, and still scared that he would leave me. I had lain there terrified that I would wake up and he would be gone, when the part of my body that had just been wrenched to pieces lay silent, too tired to even speak up and tell me to run as fast and as far from him as I could.

I feel pathetic for those last few lines and for what happened later. The fact of the matter is, however, that it is not pathetic: merely the next course of events in a pattern of abuse.

He & I had been dating for over a year. (Amazing isn't it? How long it takes to realize when you're all wrapped up in it?) I didn't realize what had really happened until just a month ago, and, suddenly, it all came rushing back: what happened to me, what he did to me exactly a year ago.

We had been off and on for about two months. It had all begun when he told me on our one year anniversary that his "life would be easier if [I] didn't exist". Happy Anniversary to meeeeeee. I should have walked, run, sprinted, skipped away then. That would have left me relatively unscathed, but, instead, I sat silent for three days and wondered what the fuck was going on.

And he told me he loved me. And he was sorry. And he was just stressed. And didn't I understand that he didn't mean it. And I thought about all the lovely gestures he had planned and executed for me in the preceding year – he was fantastic at grand gestures: scavenger hunts for gifts, great big plans, turning his room into my favorite movie for Valentine's day, writing an article about me, websites in my honor – and I fell into it. I wanted so badly to believe that it was just a bad day; so I did. I forgave him and we stayed together.

He brought me hot chocolate in the rain at the end of my work shift a few days later and expected that that would fix it all. I cried in the car and told him that what he had said to me still hurt and he took me back to my apartment and dumped me on the spot because I hadn't been grateful enough that he brought me hot chocolate. I cried. I sobbed. I sat catatonic in my room for a day, and then I picked myself up and tried to move on.

But he wouldn't let me. A few days later, he sent me an email titled, "101 things I'm thankful for about you", and I was stunned and all of my moving on went away. We were back together the next day. But I felt wrong. Something was wrong. He bought me a necklace and gave it to me on a picnic (grand gestures, remember) and I thanked him and was happy. Still, we fought about the most random and stupid things. Then we started fighting about the way he spoke to me, the way he would fight unfairly with me and call me selfish and ungrateful, the way he would threaten to just "take me back" to my apartment when he was upset like some broken toy, and I dumped him because my friends and family tried to open my eyes to what was going on. I cried. I sobbed. I sat very still and read away my pain. Then I went to work and moved slowly forward.

My best friend took me away for a weekend to try and help, and halfway through the weekend he sent me a video of his friend's baby playing with a toy I had bought for her. I melted; babies are my kryptonite. He asked me on a date and I said yes. We went to a movie. It was as it had always been, except that the experience was a stale sort of sweet that comes from too much exposure, from a moment long passed trying to be recreated. I don't remember the movie at all. I don't remember what it was. I couldn't concentrate. He held my hand on the way out. He kissed me in the park. He told me he'd never stopped loving me. He asked me to be his girlfriend again. I told him I needed the night to think about it; so much had happened. He said no, I had to decide now. I decided it was better to have him than have no chance at having him again so I said yes.

I thought about it and I couldn't figure out if I was wrong or not. He bought me a beautiful dress a few days later and sent me on a scavenger hunt through the city to find it. I smiled at his gesture and something about abuse cycle clicked in my head, but I pushed it quickly away. Then July 4th came along.

July 4th was the day before he began the summer job I had found for him. July 4th we spent together. There was a cook-out at his mom's house and it felt like the summer before, though stale and forced. We walked along the river later and watched the fireworks together. When we were walking home I realized how exhausted I was; I had been working my internship for three weeks now and it was sapping all of my energy. I wanted sleep and I told him as much. We went back to his mother's house and downstairs to his room.

I got undressed and crawled into bed to sleep while he went to the bathroom. When he came back, I was half-asleep already and laying on my right side. He turned out the light and crawled into bed. He started to kiss me and let his hands wonder. I smiled good-naturedly and told him not tonight. I was too tired, and I was in pain from the morning (sex with him had begun to hurt early on in our relationship. Another red flag of course). He stopped momentarily before beginning to kiss me and cup my breast again. I said no again, this time less good-naturedly. "No. I'm tired. Please, I want to sleep," and he kept pushing and pushing and I was so tired.

I can't explain to you how exhausted and groggy I was. I could think of nothing but sleep. I gave in. I told him fine. I figured I would just let him do his thing and I could go to sleep after. I knew from previous experience that he believed this, his pleasure and relief, to be one of my sole duties as his girlfriend. Often when we would have sex and I would not be able to continue because of the pain, he would pull out and beg me to finish him in another way, placing it as my duty. If I refused, he would leave the bed, turn on some porn, and do it himself intending for me to feel like a failure.

I thought, that night, that letting him just do his thing would be easier than continuing to fight; I could just lay there and mentally go somewhere else while I tossed in some convincing sounds here and there. Often, afterwards, I would at least manage to finagle myself some snuggles, a little bit of that love and easy affection that had prevailed early on in our relationship. Tonight was different.

Tonight when I finally consented, his demeanor changed completely. I expected some kissing, maybe some light foreplay, something. Tonight there was nothing. He took me by the wrists, sat on the edge of the bed, put me on top of him, and told me to go. All the work was mine. I was not meant to enjoy this. That was clear.

I made my grocery list in my head. I thought about what I needed to do the next day. I focused on anything and everything besides what was happening to me. I didn't understand what was happening. Had I known that THIS – not just the kind with hitting and threatening and some stranger in a back alley – was rape, I'd like to think that I would have leapt up, slapped him, and run off. But I didn't. I didn't understand. I stayed. Because he loved me, right? He'd never hurt me, right?

He finished messy and quick, pushed me off of him, tossed me sideways onto the bed, wiped himself off with a sock, put on gym shorts, and went upstairs to chat with his mom. All of this happened without a word to me and I lay there on my side, my body expelling all he had put into me, confused and silent. As he closed the door behind him, I began to softly shake, weep, and sob the likes of which I've never heard before or since rocketed out of me. There is no way he or his mother could have missed it, but no one came. I cried for a long time and then I let everything go quiet, trying to make sense of what was going on.

I picked up my book and put it down again. I stared at my phone and then I called my mom. She couldn't really hear me. I was sobbing and kept choking over and over again, "He used me and left. Mommy! He used me and left me." Eventually, I heard his footsteps on the stairs and hurried off the phone with my mother. I pulled the shirt I had yanked on around my knees, folded myself into the top left corner *of the bed, and watched him as he came in again without a word. He turned the light off and got under the covers as I sat and watched.*

I called his name softly a few times and was finally answered with a curt and annoyed, "What?"

"I need to talk to you."

"Why?"

"It's important."

He rolled over begrudgingly. "No. I have work in the morning. You're not being very supportive right now."

"It's important," I plowed ahead. His name again and then, "Really."

"Fine. What?"

I took a deep breath, "I feel used."

"Whatever," and he rolled over to go to sleep.

I sat stunned for a bit before I shifted and told him I was going to call my mom and be right back. He sighed heavily and dramatically and told me he was just going to go upstairs to sleep.

"No!" I cried. I couldn't let him leave me alone. He may have been the man who had just raped me but if he left, my ability to convince myself that he still loved and cared about me would leave swiftly with him. I lay back down. I tried to close my eyes and sleep, but sweet nothingness alluded me. I took out my iPod to try and place my thoughts within it, but he sighed and threatened to leave again. I put it away.

And so my night went.

In the morning, his mother drove him to work and me home. I called out sick at work and sat numb all day: I thought it was my fault. I truly believed that I had done something wrong, so after sitting numb and failing to process what had happened to me, I got up and proceeded to bake his favorite dessert: homemade Reese's.

He came over that night. I didn't even get a chance to give them to him because while I thought I had done something wrong, I was sure he had as well. I told him what I felt. His response? "Saying that to me disgraces all of the survivors you work with and the experiences they've had." I sat dumbstruck. We fought. He left. I was so confused and I sat on my floor with my roommates holding onto me until I fell asleep.

The next day I threw away anything that reminded me of him, tucked the experience away, and moved on.

I didn't remember until a good while later when I was talking about shitty relationships with a new friend and it all came flooding back. It felt as if no time had passed, but here I am; alive and otherwise blissfully happy, until I close my eyes and all I can think of is that night.

A year later.

I'm okay. I'm alive. I'm happy. Really really spectacularly happy. And I survived. That's what I hold onto when my brain starts up with "why me" and the woulda, coulda, shouldas.

I Survived.

Chapter 13

THE CHANGELING'S LAMENT

"Because it's not beauty
if you don't bleed."

Volunteering at THP as an O & E volunteer not only allowed me to teach and help people, but it also allowed me to meet new people and make friends. One of these friends is Shira. I often introduce Shira to people by saying, "This is the most intense person I know." Shira and I first spoke to each other when we worked a poorly organized event. The purpose of the day was meant to empower teenage girls from the inner city. The event was great and seemed to really help the young women who attended, but the organizers did not make it known that THP was present to the participants. So Shira and I talked in a separate room by ourselves about THP, sexual violence, music, and our lives.

Shira was the first survivor speaker I personally spoke to. When she explained to me that she shares her story for others, I thought, *Holy shit. We have survivor speakers and one of them is next to me now?* It just seemed so intense to me. It amazed me that a woman could be raped, and sit and talk with someone so calmly about the fact that she had been raped. I might have been naïve, but I had never experienced that before. Listening to Shira speak about survivor speaker engagements brought back memories of the survivor speaker I listened to years ago at my training when I thought to myself, *If she can do it, anyone can.*

I learned a great deal about survivor speaker engagements through Shira. Shira told me that she sits in a circle with people and tells her story. I remember thinking how strong she was to do such a thing. Shira also told me the role of the survivor speaker accompanier. The accompanier explains THP's services, introduces the speaker, and then sits down. The speaker then tells his or her story while the accompanier sits back and observes the room. The accompanier will respond to someone in the audience if need be and also answer questions that the survivor does not feel comfortable answering. I asked if people had ever made victim blaming or ignorant statements to her. Shira told me that someone once said to her, "You are so beautiful. I can totally see how you would get raped." My mouth dropped.

Shira and I continued to talk about THP and how poorly this particular event had been organized, but we made the most of our time and got to know each other a little more. We also gave some THP brochures and cards to a few people, even though I would have preferred to have handed out more. Even in bad events, it's important to always remember that one is better than none. To me, you have a successful day if one person gets a card and calls the hotline when they need help, or calls for a counseling session, or gives the card to someone they know who may need help. THP volunteers accomplish this goal and then some on every single O & E engagement.

I have never met anyone like Shira. She shocked, impressed, intrigued, and inspired me. The event finally ended, so we packed up and left. I said to Shira, "You are phenomenal for giving your time for others. You tell people your story of being raped and allow them the opportunity to ask questions. You are a leader to some people. Some people look up to you. You are strong. You actually care about people. You actually help people. You actually help heal people." She seemed appreciative, even though I don't think she was used to the compliments. She said to me, "You get it."

Shira and I volunteered and participated in a domestic violence vigil at a city police department. This particular city has at least fifty thousand residents, but the vigil only had about twenty-five participants. The majority of those twenty-five people were police officers, politicians, domestic violence advocates, Shira, and me. My friend, her two daughters, and one of her daughter's friends also attended with maybe four other citizens.

The low turnout disappointed me, but those who attended made the best of the experience. Everyone had their candles in hand as we walked around the area. After the march, everyone went back to the police department and listened to different advocates speak at the podium. It was very sad to hear about domestic violence, but also inspirational to meet people who work in the field. I was particularly struck to hear a woman recite all of the deceased victims' names, ages, and home towns in 2011. My heart sank. It made me think of all of the people who die as a result of domestic violence. I also thought about all of the domestic violence that exists but does not end in murder.

When my time came to speak, I spoke as clearly and confidently as possible. As I always do, I explained THP's services and tried my best to make people understand that THP is there for the people. I tried to make people understand that THP staff and volunteers will do anything within their power to help people. I finished and sat back down.

Once the vigil ended, a police officer wanted to talk with me. I had apparently impressed her because she had never listened to a man speak about rape. I thanked her for the compliment, but said, "This is a crime that both women and men are affected by. People say this is a woman's issue, but one could argue it is a man's issue because the majority of perpetrators are men. I would simply argue it's a human problem, but I do believe men have a huge role in reducing sexual violence."

I told this particular police officer that she could be instrumental in helping survivors heal. She had an expression on her face that I interpreted as her thinking, *What? Me? I can?* I explained to her how some victims are blamed and treated like shit after a rape or sexual assault, either by police, hospitals, friends, or family members. I told her that she can't blame them. If she ever responds to a rape, she has to respond with empathy and help that victim in any way possible. She told me she does not respond to these kinds of crimes. So I told her to train and teach her fellow cops. I told her to help them understand how to be better responders and explain how they play a big role in a victim's life.

On a different occasion, Shira and I signed up to work an event during a concert at a college. We set up our table and sat down with our THP materials. Later in the night, Shira decided to show me a poem that she had written, which at the time received over 92,000 hits online. Shira's poem, originally published in Stone Telling, is entitled *The Changeling's Lament* (Lipkin, 2011).

The Changeling's Lament

I have studied so hard
to pass as one of you.
I've spent a lifetime on it.

I have tells.
Blisters, tremors, bruises,
all the signs that I was not meant for your world,
was not meant to be contained
in your clothes,
your shoes.
I have this terribly inconvenient allergy
to cold iron.
Hives, really.
Welts.
I stand out.

When I was little,
I asked my alleged mother,
what's a girl?

She said
you,
you're a girl,
and she laced me into dresses
(that I tore off in the school parking lot,
in line for the bus).
Laced me into ballet shoes
that left blisters
and bloodied my feet
until I had calluses.
Which she had filed off,
beauticians pinning me down,
because it's not beauty
if you don't bleed.

My dancing was different.
My dancing was swaying treelike,
or launching myself across the room,
spinning madly,
but that is not what girls do,
not human girls,
not ladylike,
not contained.

And everything
is about containment
is about being delicate
and pretty
laced into corsets
whalebone stays digging into your ribs
because it's not beauty
if it doesn't hurt.

But I studied.
I pretended.

I hid the bruises
and the tics.
I hid the big dark parts of me.
I tamed my hair.
I watched my mouth.
I hid my magic.
I did not speak of such things
because we do not speak of such things –
not anger,
not homesickness,
not longing.
Not this sense
that I don't know what the hell
a human girl is
and I can tell, I can,
that everyone knows I don't belong here.
I laugh too loud;
I am too fast or slow to laugh.
I am an anthropologist in the field of girl.
I study
but none of it
ever comes
naturally.

None of it is in my nature.

I am something larger,
more fluid,
less constrained.
But I am stranded in this place.
I have had to learn how to live here.
I have tried.
So hard.

Chapter 14

ALEXIS

———

"Just one person. It really honestly just takes one positive person. One positive person can help you. And that can go a long, long way."

Alexis, like Corey, Megan, and Shira, is a survivor speaker at THP. We first met each other at one of our O & E meetings. I got the sense that she is a shy, quiet person who keeps to herself. Over time, I learned that she did not speak that much during meetings, but when she did, you knew it. Her voice is very soft and gentle yet powerful. I learned very quickly that she is compassionate, generous, thoughtful, strong, kind and loving. Her laugh is contagious and can brighten up your day instantly. I knew she was another special person.

Alexis made me die laughing the first time I spoke with her. I signed up to volunteer at a health event on a Saturday morning. I pulled up to the event and noticed there were barely any people there. As I walked in, I saw Alexis standing at the THP table by herself.

"What's up? How are ya doin? I'm Bobby," I said.

"I'm good. I'm Alexis."

"So have you had any traffic? It looks pretty dead this morning."

"Not much, but I have given out some stuff. So I hear you can cook. What are you gonna make me?"

I thought to myself, *Who the hell is this woman? I've never spoken to her and she's demanding food from me?* I started laughing and said, "Are you crazy? You're not getting anything!" I then immediately caved and said, "Okay, what do you want? I'll bring it on Wednesday."

I'll never forget one specific THP meeting we had. Every meeting begins with a check-in question. I can't remember the specific question that day, but I remember what Alexis said. She told the room that she was good and in a great place in her life. She had a kind of peace in her eyes and tone that is hard to explain through words. I remember observing the room and saw everyone looking at Alexis with admiration and smiles on their faces. It is hard to explain, but it was one of those moments that makes you realize how strong, happy, peaceful, and caring people really can be. It felt unforgettably special.

At the time, a friend of mine wanted to have an event that focused on sexual and domestic violence. She asked if I would speak about THP. I immediately accepted. I contemplated the workshops O & E presents, but I thought a survivor speaker and a discussion afterwards would be the most beneficial for the people. I thought Alexis would be the perfect person to speak. THP agreed to have the event, and Alexis agreed be the speaker. I remember feeling excited but nervous because this would be my first survivor speaker accompaniment.

Alexis and I met before the event and talked about what she needed from me. I wanted to support her in any way possible, but I needed to know how. She tells her story, answers questions, and then leaves. She told me she would give me a look when she is uncomfortable or wants to leave, and that would be my cue to wrap everything up. Alexis did not want me to leave with her because she prefers to leave alone. That is what she normally does after speaking engagements, and that was fine with me. Whatever she wanted and needed was all I needed to know. I stood up, introduced myself, briefly explained THP's services, and then introduced Alexis.

Alexis spoke to a room of about twenty people. I listened to her, but also focused on the audience in case I needed to respond to someone being triggered or becoming emotional. Everyone in the room sat with their eyes fixated on Alexis. Some had tears in their eyes. After she told her story, she opened up the floor for questions. The audience did not ask too many questions, and then Alexis gave me a look to wrap everything up. I did, but she decided to stay.

I then began a discussion and opened up the floor to more questions. I wanted the people to ask anything they wanted to know about THP, sexual violence, prevention, or anything else that they might be interested in learning. The discussion lasted about an hour. At the end of the night, the people generously gave Alexis and I a plaque. They then filled out a questionnaire and added their personal comments. All of the comments were about Alexis. The people loved her. They found her to be strong and inspirational. Alexis has always been that way to me, but I was able to see her reaching and impacting even more people. One woman had tears in her eyes. I asked if she was okay and she said yes. She told me she loved being there and especially enjoyed listening to Alexis.

Alexis was the first person I told about writing this book. I believed I was called to do this and I desperately wanted to hear her thoughts on it. She instantly supported me and said, "If you feel like you have to do it then do it, Bobby U." I asked if she wanted to contribute from the beginning. She agreed.

After a meeting one night, we grabbed a beer at a local bar and talked about all of the survivor stories I have heard and recorded thus far. Alexis told me she wanted to record her story, so we made plans to have dinner at my apartment. We ate a ton of food, drank some beer, and then began to record. This is Alexis' story:

Alexis: I was in college at the time hanging out in my friend's dorm room before work. I left to go get ready for work. There was a knock on my door while I was getting ready. I told whoever was at the door to just come in as I was getting ready for work. It was my friend's boyfriend's friend. I would call him an acquaintance vs. a friend. We knew each other in passing.

He came in. We were kickin it and chit chattin. He ended up trying to kiss me. I told him he was buggin because I had a boyfriend at the time. He kept trying and kept trying, and I was just like, "Dude, you gotta bounce. This isn't gonna happen."

He didn't leave. He backed me on my bed. He raped me. I was crying. I asked him to stop. I begged and pleaded with him to stop, but he didn't stop. When he left, I got up, got dressed, went upstairs to the community bathroom and tried to clean myself up and wipe my face off.

I didn't want to be alone at the time so I went upstairs to the fourth floor, and I went up to another friend's room. She asked me what was wrong. I didn't tell her. I just said I didn't want to be alone. So I just laid down on her bed and watched TV. He ended up finding me. He asked if he had pleased me. And then he left.

Me: The same day?

Alexis: Yeah, the same day...ummm... I clearly didn't go to work... That was it for a long time. I just continued going to school and going to work. I eventually told my boyfriend. His response was, "What the fuck was he doing in your room?"

Me: That's the first thing he said?

Alexis: That's the first thing he said. He said, "What the fuck was he doing in your room?" I remember crying after he said that. And then I didn't tell anyone else for a really super duper long time. I just continued with school.

My boyfriend lived forty-five minutes away from me at the time. The following year I was with him and we got into this HUGE fight. He drove me back to where I lived and dropped me off at these apartments that the college had rented out to the students. So I went there with my friends. Some of my friends all lived together. We all smoked a joint or a blunt or something. I don't even remember what it was. I broke down and basically tweaked.

I remember calling my mom while I was high. I was rambling and talking about how I felt about her and her husband. I told her how I felt like she would always put him over me and that she always chose his side over mine. At the end of the night I was roaming, walking down a busy street in the city. She and my grandmother found me walking down the street crying. My destination was the hospital to get some help. I remember saying in the car, "Why did he have to rape me?" That was the first time I told anyone again. And then from there I got the help that I needed, so I started going to therapy.

I remember my boyfriend called me the next day and woke me up. He was yelling at me on the phone. He was screaming, "What the fuck is wrong with you!" I was like, "Dude. I can't do this. I can't."

Me: What was he yelling at you for?

Alexis: I don't even know. Maybe I told him that I had gotten really high. I don't really remember what happened. It's all kind of fuzzy. He was just yelling at me and I was just like, "I can't. I can't do this anymore." I hung up on him and that was it. That was the end of our relationship.

Me: How did it make you feel when he reacted the way he reacted to you when you first told him?

Alexis: It hurt. I loved him, and I thought that he loved me, ya know? So I wanted the support. I wanted him to be supportive of me, console me, and want to help me. And instead he did the total opposite. He blamed me for having this man in my room. Who does that? You're supposed to love someone, care about them, and if they're hurt, you're supposed to be there for them, but he wasn't there for me.

I honestly can't remember, but I'd say I was out of school for a bit, maybe a week or so, trying to get myself together. It's kind of a blur. But I did go to therapy. I remember my mom was at an appointment at the doctor's. They called THP and I talked to someone on the hotline. So after that I've been in and out of therapy for years.

I want to say to anyone reading this: Go with whatever you think helps. I think it can take some time to find the right therapist or find the right person for you. I'm thankful I found the right person for me, and now here I am many moons later.

Me: Many moons later.

Alexis: I'm ready to fuckin rock.

Me: So you found the right therapist for you?

Alexis: Yeah. I really like her. I'm not seeing her right now though. I decided to take a break because I was on the good right path and felt like I was in a good place. So maybe I'll go back or maybe I won't. I think that she is an amazing person. I know where to go if I ever need to go back.

Me: What has your experience been like being a THP survivor speaker?

Alexis: It's been good. I really enjoy being a survivor speaker. Of course I do this because I want other people to know they're not alone and that there is help out there, but I also do it for me because it does help me at the same time. I enjoy it. I can't see myself not doing it. I can't see myself taking a break from being a survivor speaker because it's just such an important thing to me. To be able to do that and know that... I don't know... just knowing that you can do it. It says to me that I've come a long way from that girl that was in college.

Me: What have the responses been like from the speaking engagements?

Alexis: Everything has been positive. I have yet to come across anything negative. Have I come across silly questions? Yeah, but I think that just comes with the territory. That comes with anything. But I've always had positive responses from the people I've spoken to. I love it. They rock too.

Me: I remember the card you showed me the other night. I loved what the people wrote about you.

Alexis: Yeah. That's why I do it. I love that shit. I just love it.

Me: What was it about the card that got to you?

Alexis: I mean, just like the, "Thank yous", and people saying, "You're strong", and just the support. One girl said, "Your story lets me know that I'm not alone; that I can get through this." It speaks volumes. That's why I do it. Even if it's just one person. Out of all the times I've spoken, if just one person says, "Thank you. I know that I can now do this," it's all worth it.

When I first got trained to be a speaker, a girl did her presentation and told her story. She said, "If I could go back in time and change what happened, would I?" I don't want to say that I wanted this to happen to me, but it happened and it made me who I am today, and I like who I am today. I think that's where I'm at right now.

Is it a horrible, horrible thing? Yes. It should never happen to anyone, ever, ever, ever. But I can't take it back. I can't change the past. So it's become a part of me. I'm able to deal with it and it has made me who I am today. And I do like who I am, if that makes sense. I don't know if that sounds twisted or what, but that's how I feel. Does that make sense, Bobby U?

Me: Twisted? How is that twisted?

Alexis: No I'm just saying. I don't know if that makes sense. I don't know if that makes me sound twisted.

Me: If you like who you are then that's great. What the hell is wrong with that?

Alexis: I don't know... I mean... it should never happen to anyone... ever. To say, "Can I take it back?" I don't know who I'd be if that didn't happen, ya know? I know that I've changed since it happened. I know I'm a lot more guarded. I know that there are certain things that I don't like. And there's no compromising in that.

Everything has changed. Relationships are totally different. Even just small things I see on TV that someone might say. Or maybe I just hear it differently now. I'm like, "What? What did you just say? I don't think I like that. I don't like the way you're looking at her or I don't like how you're looking at him." Just little things like that. So everything changes completely.

Me: From what I've seen and the stories I've been told, there are plenty of people that don't like themselves. In fact, I've met many people who unfortunately hate themselves, often times because of this crime. So to hear you say that you like yourself is not twisted. I think it's motivational and empowering to people. It is to me.

Alexis: *Well thank you. I just… I don't know.*

Me: I remember a meeting when you told the group how you were in a really good place in your life. You might not even remember, but I remember.

Alexis: *I don't.*

Me: I don't know how. You said, "I'm fuckin good. I'm really good right now. I'm happy where I am." I wish you could have seen everyone's face. I wish you could see them watching you, listening to you, and arguably looking up to you. It was incredible to watch. I don't make this shit up.

Alexis: *Thank you, Bobby U.*

Me: I couldn't make that up. And I don't often hear that. How many times at our meetings do you hear someone say that? In the two and a half years I've been there I have yet to hear anyone say that. So to hear someone say that is really cool.

Alexis: *It definitely took time. I'm still working on myself. There are still changes I need to make about myself, but I've come a long way. I definitely wouldn't have been able to do it if I didn't have a great support system. My grandmother is incredibly supportive. She's my rock. She is seriously my rock. I love her to death. I'm her ride or die. Come hell or high water, there would be no stopping me if I had to get to her. If she needed anything on this planet I would go and find it for her. My mom is a great support system too. So I'm really lucky. I'm lucky, lucky, lucky in that aspect. And I was lucky enough to find a good therapist too.*

Me: You say you've come a long way. Do you feel comfortable explaining what that means?

Alexis: *I think from being the girl that was raped, not telling anyone, being on auto-pilot through the entire time, and being in a relationship with someone who is just a horrible person at the time. I won't say he's a horrible person now because he could have changed. I really don't know, but I hope so. And I hope he's doing well. But just dealing with all of that. Dealing with someone who is just so negative*

and is willing to talk down to you and put you down. I used to put up with all of that.

And even just dealing with home life. I had a step-father who I can't stand for the life of me. I can't stand him for the life of me. Dealing with that and putting up with a lot of crap that he's done, and then just finding strength and being like, "I can't be this person anymore. I'm better than this. I deserve better than this." And starting to find yourself. I know that there are people out there that you can trust and that do want to help you and do want to see you succeed.

And I think that is what a lot of THP is about, and a lot of people at THP. Even if they left THP, I think they'd still be the same people. But you just gotta find that, or just know that that's there. Just one person. It really honestly just takes one positive person. One positive person can help you. And that can go a long, long way.

Me: What has helped you internally and externally? Has it just been one supportive person for you that has helped you?

Alexis: I mean there are other positive people in my life, but being in therapy was super duper helpful for me. My therapist was my own personal cheerleader. When I may have said something that was fucking insane, she would call me out on my shit, ya know? I think I've had some great therapists. But at the same time, I've also outgrown some of them. So she could only help me to a certain point, and then I would start with someone else. Having a great therapist, for me, was my big thing. And also knowing my grandmother was always there no matter what. No matter what. I could be in the wrong and she would still be there. It's an unconditional love.

I don't know if I want to say "get better", but get to where I know I deserve to be. I don't deserve to sit here and cry and cry and cry all the time, be sad, not want to do anything, and just walk through life on fuckin auto pilot. It's not fair. I deserve a lot more than that. Did this person rape me? Take something from me? Yes. He took something from me that I can never ever in a million years get back. But I can get up and dust myself off. It might take me fifteen, twenty, or thirty years, but I'll get there. I'll get to where I know I can be, where I deserve to be, and where I want to be.

I think when you have positive people in your life you start to see the positive. It's like, "Ya know what? I deserve this purse. I'm gonna go buy it. Ya know what? I want to eat pizza. I'm gonna go get some fuckin pizza."

Me: You want me to go make you a pizza right now?

Alexis: Hahaha no! It might sound silly but it's things like that. It's like, "Ya know what? I don't like your tone. I don't like how you're talking to me." Dammit, say it. It's like, "Who the hell are you talking to me like this? Don't invade my personal space. Respect me cause I'm respecting you." So you get there. And you damn well better. You just stick to it. You got it. You got to. Yeah. That's right, Bobby U.

Me: Is there anything you want to say to people about you? About this crime? About the impacts of it? About healing? About anything?

Alexis: I would say to the person that raped me...and he knows who he is...well, let me back up. I get asked a lot, "If I ever saw this person again, what would I say? How would I react?" I can say right now I'd be fine and I would just walk out of the room and that's it. It's a part of my life that I have moved past and I just want to keep moving forward. But honestly, I feel like right now I'd be like, "Ya know what mothaa fuckaa, we're taking this to the streets. We're taking it to the fucking streets. Knuckle up." He might beat me up, or I might beat him up, but damn well I'll probably fight dirty. Let's be real.

I'm not saying physical violence is the answer. It never is. But, I guess the only thing I can think of is that you're just a piece of shit. You're worse than a piece of shit. You're a parasite. You're nothing. You're just a horrible, horrible individual. I don't even know if I feel sorry for you. You're just disgusting. You're nothing. You're...I don't even know a word that I can think of that's even good enough to describe what I think you are, because I think that you're just that horrible. And you deserve nothing. And you should be sent straight to hell and have your hairs plucked one by one with a tweezer.

But then again, sometimes I do feel bad for you because you feel like you have to take these things from someone, or from people, to make you feel better. You know what you're doing. You're a grown ass man. You know better. You know right from wrong.

I would say to other survivors: You're strong. There is help out there. When you're ready to seek it, or get it, or receive it, it's there. And if you told anyone and they've given you a negative or nasty response, I guess depending on whom that person is to you, you need to cut them out of your life because you don't need that. You don't fucking need that. And I can honestly say that anyone who would give me a negative response wouldn't be in my life. You're supposed to love me. I don't need that. I don't deserve it. Neither do you. And maybe you feel like someone believes something negative about your story or blames you. Tell them to keep that shit to their fucking self. Don't bring it over to you.

People need to respect that person. Respect them and just be there for them and give them whatever support they might need. Maybe they just need to talk. Maybe they want responses. Maybe they just want to cry. Maybe they just want you to sit there and shoot the shit. If that is true then you do that for them no matter what. If it's fucking five o'clock in the morning, three o'clock in the morning or two o'clock in the afternoon, you do it for them because that's what they need at the time. Something that small can help them for miles and miles and miles and miles.

There are people there that can help you and you will get through it. You'll never get over it, but you will get through it and you'll learn. You'll learn, I guess I want to say, to live it. You'll learn to know that it's a part of you. But you're better than that. And even though it is a part of you, it doesn't have to consume you.

Me: It doesn't have to define you?

Alexis: It doesn't define you at all by any means. It maybe changed you. Definitely. But you'll get through it. You will. I guess whatever makes you feel better. If it's your faith that gets you through it, or a best friend, or your therapist, or maybe it's dance. Just something. Whatever motivates you. Whatever speaks to you that helps you do it and get through it: use them. Whatever it is. If it's THP, or whatever rape crisis counselor it is, or a teacher, or whomever. What else ya got, Bobby U?

Me: I'd love for this book to be a healing guide for people. Hopefully they can read it and think, *Oh I can do this. I can try this. This might work.* Is there a set way to heal? Or is it just really different for different people?

Alexis: I think it's absolutely different for everyone. It's definitely different for every single person. Someone's thing might be painting, and that's how they express their sadness and anger and all the above. They can zone out and paint. I can't fucking draw a circle. I would love to paint. As a matter of fact I'm going to sign up for painting, but I'm just doing it because I'm like, "Let's try it. It might be fun." I think for someone that can actually be their thing. That's what gets them through it. Or even exercising. Whatever it might be.

Me: You've always told me people will seek out help when they are ready. What does that mean?

Alexis: It means that you'll know when you're ready. It might sound silly, but it's like how someone says, "How do you know when you're ready to marry someone?" You just know. You know. Maybe you're head over heels in love with this person. You can't stop thinking about them. If they ever left your life you'd be sad. I don't know. But they say that you just know. And I think for me, getting high and having my mom and grandmother finding me wandering down the street was it for me. It couldn't get any lower for me.

And having a boyfriend who treated me like crap for years and years prior to that, I couldn't get any lower to where I already was. I was just ready. I was ready to make that turn and seek the help that I needed because I was clearly headed down a path of destruction. I was headed down a path of self-destruction. I didn't want that. I don't think anyone wants that.

Me: How powerful is it when someone listens to a survivor? When someone believes and validates a survivor?

Alexis: I can't speak for all, but for me it was just like, "Thank you." Just a big, "Thank you. Thank you for being there. Thank you for listening." Even if it's a fucking stranger, because sometimes that's exactly what it is. It's a stranger. And you just want to be heard. And it hurts so badly when someone that you care about isn't hearing you and isn't supporting you. But when you finally find that one, or two, or whomever, I feel like it's just such a relief. You start to peel off that layer. It will take some time, but it is one day at a time. I'm heading in the right direction. Bobby U listened to me today.

Me: I'll always listen to you.

Alexis: I'm just saying, like, Bobby U listened to me today. Tomorrow's another day. And I feel a lot better today. And if I can feel better today then I know I can feel better tomorrow.

Me: What does "empowerment" mean to you?

Alexis: I guess it's allowing me to make my own decisions. I'm gonna do whatever the hell I wanna do. You're not gonna tell me I need to do this. If I tell you, "Hey, this just happened to me", I don't need you to say, "You need to do this." I don't have to do anything I don't wanna fucking do. I'm talking to you because I want to share this with you. Just shut up and listen. If I want to know your opinion about, "Hey I just cut my finger. What do you think I should do?" then you can offer me your opinion. But until then I suggest you shut the hell up. That's what empowerment is to me. Just listening and allowing me to make my own decision. You can make suggestions, but don't tell me I need to do something. I don't need to do a goddamn thing. I just need to stay black and die. That's it.

Me: Stay black and die?

Alexis: That's it. That's all I need to do.

Me: How can other people become empowered? How can other people grow?

Alexis: I can't... I don't know. That's a really difficult question because everyone is different. And I would just like to say: You do what you want to do. If you're like, "Ya know what; I don't want to be in therapy. Someone's making me go to therapy, forcing me to go to therapy." Then fine...go...leave therapy. Do what you want to do. Be the person who you want to be. That's it.

I'm sorry... I should get off my soap box. I feel like I'm on a soap box.

Me: You should what?

Alexis: I feel like I'm on a soap box. I'm just like, "You go do what you wanna do."

Me: You can talk as much as you want, but we can also shut this down. I'm wondering, is there one final thing you would like to say to people for them to take away from this? When they walk away reading this book, and they have this with them, what would that be? What is one simple message you can give people?

Alexis: One simple message? I have more than one simple message.

Me: So then give them more than one simple message.

Alexis: Of course what I say all the time: You fucking rock. You take that away. You fucking rock and let's rock. Those two things. That's it. And this might sound silly, but if no one believes you, if that's how you feel that no one believes you, I fucking believe you. You can talk to me through this book, and Alexis is fucking listening to you and is there with you and is supporting you. And whatever it is you wanna do I'm supporting you in that. That's it. There is someone. I might not know you or know what you look like, but know I'm with you in spirit. Or whatever you believe, know that I'm right there with you. I believe you. So let's fucking rock. Because you rock, and I rock, and we're rocking together.

Chapter 15

JIM

———

"He would come into the classroom and tell the nun he wanted to see me. He took me out into the hallway, into a different room, and gave me a cigarette. The both of us were just sittin there havin a cigarette shootin the breeze."

I'll never forget the first time I met Jim. I signed up for a survivor speaker engagement and later learned I would accompany a male survivor. I didn't even know THP had male survivor speakers. I was shocked and intrigued. Jim turned out to be the first and only man I ever accompanied who spoke openly about his rape through THP.

Jim and I agreed to grab a coffee to meet and become better acquainted with each other. I got there a little early, so I called Jim to let him know I had arrived. As soon as I picked up the phone, I could tell he had grown up in eastern Massachusetts because of his thick accent. I could instantly see how nice and gentle of a man he is once we met.

We introduced ourselves and talked about the upcoming engagement as Jim bought me a coffee. He stressed to me that he really wants to help people. Talking about his rape helps him in his healing process, but his other objective is to help others. I was in awe as we continued to have a conversation. I told Jim that I would explain THP's services and then let him speak. I emphasized to him that he should say whatever he wanted. Jim said that he would stay late and speak with anyone if they wanted to ask him questions. I thought that was great and told Jim I would stay late to support him and talk to others as well.

Jim proceeded to tell me that he had been sexually abused by a Catholic priest at the parish he served as an altar boy. "Who is worse? The priest who abused me or the other priest who walked in and did nothing?" Jim asked me. I was blown away by that question. I didn't have an answer, nor was he looking for one.

We talked about his family reactions and how his siblings wanted to kill the priest who abused him. We also discussed the Catholic Church and Irish and Italian Catholic families. We ended the conversation and then parted ways. I thanked him for being the person he is and walked away inspired. I thought Jim was incredibly strong, brave, and caring. I couldn't wait for his speaking engagement.

Jim spoke to students and parents at a high school a few days later. Everyone focused very intensely on Jim. I could see that he reached some of the men, women, and adolescents in the crowd that night. After his speech and a round of questions, Jim and one woman talked with each other for over a half hour. A year later, I spoke at a college to parents about how sexual violence affects adolescents. Two of the participants had been in attendance a year prior and heard Jim's speech. They said the people in attendance really loved Jim. One woman said Jim was all she could think about for a week.

I knew that I wanted Jim to share his story for this book, but I wasn't sure if he felt comfortable or not. Jim responded to my request and seemed happy to contribute. We grabbed a coffee for a second time and discussed the book. I asked him if he felt more comfortable writing or speaking. He wanted to speak, so I told him I would buy a recorder. I invited Jim to my apartment to have a home cooked Italian meal and some wine. I had the peaceful piano playing on my ipod throughout the night to help put Jim at ease. Jim is tough as hell, but talking about his rape is difficult, as it is for anyone I have ever met. After we ate, he moved to my reclining chair while I sat on the couch. This is the conversation we had. This is Jim's story:

Me: So, Jim. Thank you so much for doin this. I give you a ton of credit.

Jim: My pleasure.

Me: And ahhh, please…whatever you ahhh…

Jim: I have to give a little bit of the background with my family. I was one of six, and I was right in the middle. I had a terminally ill mother who was in dialysis three days a week. My father was a police officer who worked most of the time. He had to take care of a sick wife and six kids. This kind of sets the stage in how the family dynamic was goin on at the time.

I used to look for attention like any kid would look for attention because it really wasn't in my home. My mom couldn't give me much attention because of all of the dealings she had goin on. It wasn't really there with my dad because he wasn't around. So I found it outside of the family, and in particular, one priest who took a specific interest in me for a long period of time.

As an adult looking back on it, I can see it was the whole grooming process that was goin on, in terms of bein an altar boy when I was in Catholic school, and bein named the head altar boy by this particular priest cause he was in charge of all the altar boys, and bein able to make my own schedule for the masses. I thought it was pretty cool that I would give myself the 4pm mass on a Saturday afternoon as opposed to 7am mass on a Sunday morning. Ya know, stuff like that.

I remember him when I was in the 8th grade. He would come into the classroom and tell the nun he wanted to see me. He took me out into the hallway, into a different room, and gave me a cigarette. The both of us were just sittin there havin a cigarette shootin the breeze. Looking back on it… Who in their right mind would pull an 8th grade student out of their classroom to have a cigarette with him? It's just…

Me: No one noticed? No one…

Jim: They noticed. They MUST have noticed. But nobody said anything about it. I remember that distinctly. We we're just sittin there. We would be havin a conversation and he would just give me a cigarette, and he would light it up for me. I believe the principal, nun, and everybody else in the school knew what was goin on, yet nobody said anything about it. I don't know that for a fact, but they had to be absolutely blind to not see what was goin on there. In this day and age, you wouldn't be takin a kid outta the school and havin a cigarette with him and just shootin the breeze. They're in the middle of class when they're supposed to be in there learning. There were a lot of interactions like that.

I was really involved with the church, the parish, and all the activities they had goin on, such as the CYO. The church used to have a Christmas fair every year, so we used to help set up for the Christmas fair and work the Christmas fair. We used to set up for their New Year's Eve parties and sit at the table with everyone. I just immersed myself into the church because that's the way I was raised; you go to church, and you become part of the church and the church becomes part of you.

And then on one evening, he asked me to meet him in the rectory. It was after dinner because it was dark outside. It was probably somewhere around 7pm. He invited me into his room and gave me a beer. At the time I was in the 8ᵗʰ grade. So at the time it would put me at what? Thirteen years old or somewhere right around there? We were in there and I thought it was the coolest thing, ya know? Here I am with a priest and he's givin me a beer. And I'm in his room at night, in the rectory, not seeing all of the red flags that are goin up all over the place.

During the middle of the conversation there was a knock on the door. The priest who was next door asked him to step out into the hallway. He closed the door, but I could hear both of them arguing. I couldn't pick up a lot of what they were sayin, but the one thing that did stick out in my mind is the other priest sayin, "He shouldn't be here. He shouldn't be in the rectory at this time of night. Kids shouldn't be allowed in your room at ANYTIME during the day, let alone at night." After that the priest came back in, and the other one went back to his room, and that was it. So he KNEW what was goin on, and he confronted my molester to say I didn't belong there, yet, I was still there and he went back to his room and nothing else was said about it.

So at that point we had one beer. Then we had a second beer. And then he took off his shirt and asked me to stand up. And I stood up, and he was getting really close to me. He started to rub himself in his private parts and asked me to step over to the bed. After that is where everything else just went blank. I just couldn't remember a thing. But after it was over, and I left the room, there is a part that I'll never forget. It's just seared into my memory. I walked back out of his room down the hallway, and the priest who he had the confrontation with earlier had his door open. I looked in as I was goin by, and he looked at me, and he just had the saddest look I've ever seen on anybody's face.

Me: He had the saddest look?

Jim: He had the saddest look. I'll never forget it. I'll never forget the look.

Me: Why?

Jim: I didn't understand it at the time because I didn't know what had happened, but I knew something was really wrong. Something very, very wrong happened. I could feel it in my gut that something very, very bad happened.

Me: Do you think he felt remorse for not stepping in and doing something?

Jim: Absolutely. I think that's where the look was comin from. The one thing I do remember this priest sayin is, "Don't tell anybody you were here tonight." He said, "So if you tell somebody you were here tonight I will just deny it, so don't tell anybody." I went home, and

I was just feelin that something was really wrong. I wanted to tell somebody, but I was scared to death to tell somebody because I was told not to. And at that point I just buried it. I buried it for decades. I didn't think about it at all.

There is a second piece that came out that really blew my mind, and this memory just came back recently over the last couple of years. In the days after bein molested, I felt a really bad pain in my butt area. It was really bad. My mom thought it was hemorrhoids, so she said, "Go down to the store and get some Preparation H." So I got Preparation H, but that wasn't working at all. The pain was a pain I've never felt before, so she took me to the doctors. I was in the room with the doctor and he did an examination. At the end of the examination, he looked me dead in my eye and he said, "I don't know what you're doin down there, but whatever you're doin ya better stop it because you're gonna hurt yourself." I had no idea what he was talkin about because my mind went blank after I went over to the priest's bed.

First off, he was a trained professional, so he knew somethin was goin on. He must have known somethin was goin on. Or, at the time, maybe he didn't have the training or the knowledge to know what was goin on or what to look at. Maybe people didn't believe that it happened to boys as well as girls.

The second piece of it is, what did he tell my mother after he left that room? Ya mom takes ya to the hospital for a certain reason, yet, he says that to me. I had no idea what he said to her because she said absolutely nothing to me. It's something that I can't go back and discuss with her because she passed away back in 1993. It's just something that I have to live with sayin, "what if", ya know? Did she know somethin and try to cover it up? Or did the doctor not tell her what was really goin on and what he said to me? Even if I did have knowledge of it, after that comment, I wouldn't have said anything to anybody at that point. I just wouldn't have done it. Not in a million years.

So for me, the memories started to come back in 2003. The memory coming back of actually bein in the rectory came up cause somebody came up to me one time and said, "You're giving classic signs of somebody who's been sexually abused."

Me: What does that mean?

Jim: In terms of the fight or flight. Always bein very angry. The passive aggressive behavior that goes on in a relationship: "I wanna be here, I don't wanna be here. I wanna be here, I don't wanna be here." Bein very awkward in social situations. Just not feelin comfortable in my own skin. Just... ya know... everything.

It coulda been that or it coulda been something else, but as I started to think about it a little bit more, some of these memories started to come back and I was sayin, "Why was I in that room in the rectory that night," and "Why did that priest come over and start to talk," and "Why was my butt really sore?" I started to put two and two together and said, "Oh my God. Something like this happened to me."

I really didn't wanna tell anybody then because I couldn't recall everything that was goin on. People are gonna say, "Well, if you had something that traumatic happen, how can you not remember it?" That played mind games with me for years. It really did. Until one day I got up enough guts to go looking for that priest, the one who was in the room next door. I found out that he was still alive.

Me: Where did you find him?

Jim: He was in a retirement home. So I called him up one day and I said, "Do you mind if I come down to talk to you?" I told him who I was and he said, "Yes, I remember who you are." He said, "Sure. You can come on down." So I walked in his room. He was probably in his mid-eighties with failing health. He was using an oxygen tank. So the first words outta my mouth was, "I came here to talk to you about Father O'Donnell." He responded back and said, "Well ya know he's dead, right?"

Me: That's the first thing he said?

Jim: *Yeah. I said, "Yeah I know he's dead. I recalled he died back in the early 80s." He said, "Well why don't ya just let him rest in peace." I just looked at him. It was just the way he said it and the way he looked at me, and I said, "Do you remember that night in that rectory?" And he said, "Just let him rest in peace."*

I'm just lookin at the guy in his mid-eighties who coulda ulti-mately stopped it all those years ago. Do I really wanna go at it with somebody who is not gonna talk? I wanted to put my fist right through him, but where is that gonna get me? It's not gonna get me anywhere. As far as I'm concerned, he can live with the guilt, assuming he even feels any guilt at all. Hearing him say, "Just let him rest in peace" as the first thing that came outta his mouth was like bein re-victimized all over again. I said, "I came to talk to ya, to try to put some closure to this, and this is the way you're gonna respond? You're gonna just put the wall right up."

After that interaction I tried to get some help. I found a therapist. This was the same time the whole Catholic Church sex abuse scandal started to blow up. I found that this particular individual special-ized in male sexual abuse. So I went to talk to him, but most of our sessions were dealt with me listenin to him and his problems with his partner, as opposed to him listenin to me. Plus I was up here in my head (Jim pointing to his head) *and I wasn't down here in my heart. I was goin through the motions thinkin I was really helpin myself when I really wasn't.*

That lasted maybe a couple of months, and then my brother died. After that happened I just stopped goin to therapy and thought that I could just push the whole thing down and not deal with it. I would just keep doin what I've been doin my whole life because it got me to a certain point. It got me to that day and age, but things started to come up where the way I dealt with it before just wasn't workin anymore. Too many emotions were comin up and I was tryin to push em back down. I was goin crazy. I had to deal with all my shit.

About three years ago I went through a simple procedure. I had my gallbladder taken out. After the procedure, I had a blood clot that went to my lung when I was at my house. They rushed me back to the hospital and I was lucky. I was sittin in the hospital room at night by myself dealing with that and thinking that it coulda easily went the other way. I was considering how lucky I was, and I ended up making two decisions that night. The first decision was to start the process of adopting, which ultimately came true. And then the second decision was to finally deal with the sexual abuse. I had to deal with it. It was just eatin me up on the inside at that point.

So that's where I came in contact with THP. Maddie, the counselor at THP, was great. You ever watch the show, "The Biggest Loser"? She was like my Jillian Michaels. She was tough as nails. She would ask me a question and I would dance all around the question, and eventually she would just pull me back in and say, "You gotta do this." And that's what I really needed at that point in time. I needed somebody to hold my feet to the fire and say, "Ya know, you gotta deal with this" and "How does it feel?"

And then it all came to a head one day. There were two things that people could say about me. Number one, I never cried. Never did. Just never happened for me. As much as I tried, I just couldn't do it. And the second thing is I have always been told I look so serious all the time. They would say, "Why don't ya lighten up? Ya look so serious." People have been tellin me that since I was a kid.

I was participating in group therapy with Maddie and something crazy happened one day. I was just drivin down the expressway, and all of a sudden everything just came up. I just had a complete breakdown in the middle of the expressway while goin to work. This had never happened to me before. I said, "I can't go to work like this. There's just no way." I was a basket case.

Me: What happened?

Jim: All this emotion just came up.

Me: Out of nowhere? Did something trigger it?

Jim: Yeah, somethin did trigger it. We had a group session the night before. We were talkin about compassion, and having compassion for yourself. It was just the way it was said; it just resonated with me for some reason. It just stuck with me that whole night. And the next day when I was driving to work I was just thinking about it, and all of the emotions just came up. I was bawlin my eyes out while being stuck in bumper to bumper traffic. I said, "I gotta get the fuck outta here." It was just the weirdest thing.

I called my partner and told him what was goin on. He said, "You want me to come home?" I said, "No, I really need to be by myself right now." I needed to allow myself to go through this because I knew it was a breakthrough. All those years of holdin it down and pushin it down was beginning to come up. If it wasn't for goin to THP and havin Maddie holdin my feet to the fire, I never would have got to the point that I am today. Not in a million years.

I was workin with Maddie and I was like a scared little boy, even though at the time I was a forty-five year old grown man. Looking back on just a year, where I was back then to where I am right now, it's just light years. Light years different. We even kid about it when we see each other from time to time.

It's encouraging to know that there's people out there who do care. There's people out there who are willing to help. There's services out there that can help you, but you have to be willing to take that first step. If you don't take that first step, then you'll just be stuck in the shame, sorrow, negativity, and just all the nasty side of what the abuse has to offer.

Me: How many years did you stay silent for?

Jim: I would say from 1978 up to 2003. About twenty-five years.

Me: Did you tell your family?

Jim: I told my family. I was thinkin about it and I said, "I'm ready to take that step to let people know what had happened." I wanted to do it one by one, but knowin my family, bein from a large family,

I knew that if I tell one they'll automatically be on the phone to the other one, and I didn't want it to happen that way. I wanted them to hear it from me. But if ya drop a bomb that big, I know they're gonna be callin each other up.

So I decided to do it by email. After I wrote the email and sent it out to them, I said the only thing I'm looking for right now is just your support and your love, and I know you'll be there for me. I heard from every single one of them either on the phone or on email within twelve hours. Every single one. So it spread throughout the whole family, and then to the extended family with my aunts and uncles.

Me: Were they supportive of you?

Jim: Every single one of them. My older brother was so upset. He just wanted to go kill someone. I said, "No, you don't wanna kill anybody. You got three small girls at home. So you don't wanna go and do somethin stupid." My two aunts were ex-nuns in the Catholic Church. They called me up one day. You ever see that show the Golden Girls where they have both women on the phone? My aunts were both on the phone cuttin me up with questions back and forth.

They were like, "When did this happen!" I said, "Ahhh, I think it happened at this time." They screamed, "Well who's the pastor! It better not have been that priest because Jesus Christ if I find out it was him! He would NEVER allow kids up on the second floor; I know that for a fact he would never allow kids up there!" I said, "Well, whoever was there at the time allowed the kid up on the second floor because I was that kid."

They were askin me questions about my faith and how it has affected me with my faith. Now…today…I'm more upset with the Catholic Church than I think I've ever been in my entire life. I just got a bad taste in my mouth about it. I think I just kinda put up a front all those years. I haven't lost my spiritual side of me, but it's just the whole Catholic Church, makin sure you have to do this at this time and this at that time. I think they are hypocrites about pretty much everything right across the board. How they knew this was goin on, had proof that they knew this was goin on, and just moved pedophiles from one parish to another parish to another parish to another parish; it just blows my mind.

Me: And Law is currently in Rome, right?

Jim: Yup.

Me: Cardinal Law is still in Rome.

Jim: He's still in Rome. Cardinal Law happened to be the person at the throne at the time it happened. It coulda been Cardinal Cushing. It coulda been Cardinal Meideros. It coulda been any single one of them goin right up the line. And ya even had Pope Benedict XVI who was John Paul's right hand man, who was dealin with all this abuse in the Catholic Church that was goin on. Do I have first-hand knowledge of it? No. But does my gut tell me he knew something was goin on? Absolutely. To me it starts right up at the very top and goes all the way down. How could ya not know when ya have it happenin in so many different countries? Ya can't be that disconnected from the folks below ya not to know that. Ya just can't be.

Me: So how did it make you feel when you received so much support from your family?

Jim: It made me feel loved. It was weird because we grew up in a very dysfunctional family. But I always had that safe feelin that if somethin happened to one of us, everybody else would circle the wagons and rally around that person. And that's exactly what happened. Regardless of whatever disputes we had goin on, or the petty little shit, if something major happened, ya knew that they would have ya back. Absolutely have ya back.

Me: Are there things that hurt you in the healing process? Are there things that helped you in the healing process?

Jim: The worst part of the healing process for me was actually opening up and tellin people. Even though I know that's part of the healing process, but that was also the most difficult part for me. When I went to the group, I used to just sit there and listen to everybody else talk, but not really add too much until I was prompted to. And then I would answer the question of whatever was goin on at the time. But

I found out that as I continued down that road and the more I talked about it, the more the recovery got a little bit better and a little bit stronger.

But there was a period of about a year that was the worst year of my life. I wasn't sleepin. I just wasn't myself at all because of all this emotion from the past trauma. Everything was comin out at the same time. And really what I wanted to do was put a lid back on it and go back to the way I was livin my life before I decided to deal with it, because once that can of words was open, forget it. It just comes flooding out. But I know that without doing that I wouldn't be where I am today. Ya have to go through it. Ya have to go through it.

Me: And where are you today?

Jim: I'm in a much better place now. Much, much better place. I'm speakin out more about it. I speak about it publicly. I'm helpin out with ya book. I spoke to my boss about it and he was really supportive. I spoke with the executive director of a non-profit. So I'm in a much better place.

Me: Is there anything that you want people to know about sexual violence? Healing? What it means to stay silent and not speak? Is there anything else you want to say?

Jim: I think out of all the things that can happen to a person in their lifetime, I would say bein sexually abused as a child and having your innocence taken away, to me, is at the top of the list. And I'm not sayin that just because it happened to me. I'm sayin it because when you're a child, you're expected to be a kid. Adults in authoritative roles, whether it is a priest, police officer, teacher, or coach, there's a level of trust there that the adults are supposed to take care of the kids. And that didn't happen in my case.

But as I went through the recovery and noticed that even the worst possible thing that can happen to a person, there is still good that can come outta that. It helped me be me. It's a part of me. It's who I am today. I wouldn't be where I am today without havin that. People ask me, "Did you wish that didn't happen to you?" And I always say, "No.

I wouldn't wanna change a thing that happened to me in my life. It helped me shape the person I am today."

It also gave me a renewed hope in people. Even outta the very worst, very good things can happen, regardless of where you are in the spectrum. There's still really bad things that are goin on today, but more and more people are speakin about it. When you think about some of the statistics that are out there, that some believe that one outta every four girls and one outta every six boys will be sexually assaulted in their lifetime...that's a pretty big fuckin problem in this country. It's huge. And to sit back and know that it goes on and not say anything about it is just criminal. It's absolutely criminal. It needs to be put out there for all of the people's faces, because I believe that's the only way you're gonna get change to happen.

Ya got the Catholic Church sexual abuse scandal. Ya got what happened at Penn State. And that's just people in trusted places.

Me: That's also just what we know.

Jim: Yeah.

Me: That's just what comes out in the media.

Jim: Yeah. You have no idea what goes on in people's families. In their own families.

Me: No idea.

Jim: I don't rank them or rate them in any way, shape, or form. For me, I had the ability to have a family that was very supportive when I think about it and tell them. But can you imagine if it was somebody in the family who did it? If someone sexually assaulted me and then I try to tell the rest of the family? The turmoil that would cause? And that's what a lot of people face now a days. When it comes out, a lot of times people don't have their family to fall back on. That's why I keep going to places like THP and other networks and organizations. Whether it is web-based, or even go there in person, they're really there to help people out.

Me: Is there anything else that you want to add?

Jim: Yeah. I think I just said it, but I think it's worth repeating. They gave me hope that there is good in the world out there. There really is. It really does exist. Regardless of how bad things can be, and how down on your luck you can be, or how bad your trust is broken when it comes to warming up to people and all that stuff, I know that there's people out there that genuinely wanna help. Putting yourself in that position is a huge step, and it's a very risky and fragile step, but it's also a step that needs to be taken because there is help. And you can get through something like this. You really can.

You can have the shame taken away. You can go from bein awkward in social situations, from beatin yourself up with negative talk and everythin right across the board, to comin out the other side and standin on your own two feet. You can feel comfortable in your own skin, have your confidence come back, have your self-esteem come back, and see everything that's good about the world. That does exist out there, even through something as very, very dark as this. There is hope on the other side. There really is.

Chapter 16

DON

———

"This is why I never finished college. This is why I'm an alcoholic. This is why I've had some sexual problems. This is why I've had depression. This is why, this is why, this is why."

Jim called me with a request about a week after he came to my apartment to share his story. He asked if he could speak to his male support group to find out if there were members who wanted to contribute to this book. I loved the great idea, but I wondered if anyone would be interested or felt comfortable enough to come forward. I thought, *Would men I've never met before talk about their sexual abuse and their life to a complete stranger? No way.* Turns out I could not have been more wrong. Two men told Jim they would like to speak with me. Jim connected us over email and we began to communicate. The first man who reached out was Don.

Don and I exchanged a few emails and spoke briefly on the phone. He planned to come to my apartment on a Friday morning around 9am to share his story. That morning was the first time I had ever met Don. I did not know it at the time, but this would be the first time he had ever shared his whole story with someone during one sitting. Neither one of us knew what would come out or what to expect from each other. This is Don's story:

Don: So…my story…boy I don't even know where to begin… Ahhh…I was sexually abused (digitally raped) at four years old. I had no idea this happened until I was in my mid-fifties, so it was literally one-half a century that I had repressed it.

However, there were a few small events in my life which in hindsight were clues. I was at a men's gathering about twenty years ago and we did an age regression exercise. I figured I would stop at age twelve since that's when I had a major blow-up with my parents, but I kept going back until age four. Why stop at four? Then we had to draw a picture and I drew a kid, me, sitting on a bed looking out a window. It was the saddest thing I've ever seen (or felt) in my life. We had to tell what the drawing was about, but I could not speak and had to do all I could do to keep from crying. I did not have a clue what the hell was going on. No clue at all.

Another time, I saw the movie, "Dolores Claiborne". One of the characters discovers near the end that she had been sexually abused by her father when she was young. Nothing specific rang a bell, but I was very sad, melancholy for two or three days, but again, had no clue why. With great 20/20 hindsight, I know now.

Me: Do you recall when the flashbacks started?

Don: I was about fifty-five or fifty-six. My wife and I were walking down the street after dinner. My wife reached out to touch my hand, just to hold my hand, and I had like a shock reaction. I wanted to pull my hand away – it was like being touched by a live electrical wire, and the word "rape" came to me. I pretended I had an itchy head and pulled my hand away. I was almost panic struck and had no idea what was happening to me. That was the beginning of the flashbacks. The only way I can understand any of this is that my Higher Power let me remember when I was ready and not a moment sooner.

The memories began, sometimes slowly and sometimes quicker. They just popped up when they popped up. I now knew something had happened and I started having mini-panic attacks. Thank God I had a therapist who knew what was going on. With the flashbacks, I knew something had happened, but it was not until the fall of 2005 (I was fifty-eight) when I really began to put a lot more of the pieces together and know who the perpetrator was – my quiet uncle.

I was really shocked, but I knew in my gut I was right. This guy was ultra-quiet and I rarely saw him even though we lived in the same area of town. I would see him in church or at an occasional family function. Around 2000, I ran into him at the RMV. I stood a couple of feet away from him and had a five to ten minute conversation. I couldn't believe I was that close to the guy and did not know he raped me! I really must have buried the memories pretty deep. Again, I was lucky enough to have a qualified therapist who helped explain how this stuff works. Actually, it was three months after his death that I knew it was him. He had to be dead for me to feel safe enough to remember.

Another "peculiar" memory: a year or two later, I came home from work and I saw some Christmas wreaths and fir branches on the back porch. I knew that my wife was about to decorate for the Christmas season and I felt a little perturbed, like most other Christmas times. I just said to myself, "What's the big deal?" That night she had the mantel decorated and I told her it looked good, and I really meant it. A couple of nights later, I came home and she had all the elves, holly, and every other decoration imaginable all over the place. I felt this enormous and fearful rage arise inside and I knew this had nothing to do with decorations. I immediately made up an excuse to walk to the store just to get the hell out of there.

While walking around the block, I realized the rape occurred at Christmas. I knew sometimes that as an older child, we would sometimes see him Christmas night at my grandmother's. A couple of weeks later, I went to my mother's place that had several photograph albums. I found this scrapbook, and on Christmas Eve, 1951, there was a picture of my uncle in my parents' kitchen. I didn't really need any confirmation, but there it was in a photo. I still get a little uneasy just talking about it.

Another flashback occurred at my therapist's office. Near the end of the session, I heard the next client enter the waiting room and the door click shut behind her. The sound of the click scared the shit out of me and I just lost it. The click meant he was coming again.

Me: Was the sound of the door a trigger?

Don: Exactly! Scary as all hell! I started doing some primal therapy which is all from the neck down. The therapist would have me pay close attention to my body. I would regress back to my early childhood and sort of re-experience the rape, but in a safe place. It was freeing, and it also reinforced that it had happened more than once.

Me: Do you think someone knew?

Don: Yeah, I do. How could they not? I have an image of one of those kid's books with the golden spines, lying in my bed. That image just gives me the creeps. He was probably offering to read me bedtime stories; he was not the type to read stories. My therapist said that if the abuse happened more than once, then the odds are pretty good someone knew.

My mother and I have been butting heads forever. I was an angry child to say the least. Now I know why. I was constantly getting in trouble, again around four or five, doing things like throwing a beer bottle and rocks through the kitchen window, getting in fights, always injuring myself with reckless behavior such as falling off stone walls and knocking myself unconscious. Several times I had to be brought to the doctor to get stitched up. "Doc C. says he has never put as many stitches in any child as he has you." I heard that ad nauseum. I always thought my mother deemed me the devil child and my behavior certainly was less than a "nice" boy, so that was a problem. But a therapist wondered aloud if my mother was aware of the abuse and perhaps blamed me. I have no idea and I guess it doesn't really matter. Around pre-puberty, I began to turn all this anger inward.

Me: So you never told them?

Don: *God no! By the time I remembered, my father was long dead and my mother was in her early eighties with symptoms of dementia. Neither of my parents were very open to talking about "real" things. It's also difficult for me to talk about it because it affects my family. My uncle has long since died so he's not going to hurt anyone, but me telling my story would certainly hurt his wife and kids. I did tell both my sisters and my oldest cousin in case they, or someone they knew in the family, had been abused. None of them seemed to know how to handle it.*

That's a major problem with me: the damned isolation. I can't tell you how many hundreds (literally) of nights I sat in a darkened room, on the floor at 3am with a glass of bourbon in one hand and a cigarette in the other, just sitting there wondering what the matter was. Later I found out I was an alcoholic and I've been lucky enough to be sober a long time. I was sober twenty-five years when I began to remember. I thought I drank like that only because I had the alcoholic gene, but I also had a reason. I now know why: I was drowning my sorrows. It was too bad I didn't know what those "sorrows" were earlier so I could have begun to deal with them earlier. But like I said, I remembered when I was supposed to, i.e., when I could begin to handle it.

(Long pause)

Where do you want me to go now?

Me: Where do you feel comfortable going right now? Where do you want to keep going? You can go wherever you want. You can talk more about the recovery process if you want.

Don: *Those questions you gave me as a guide. You used the word "crime". It is a very accurate word. Sexual abuse is a fucking crime and a fucking shame. Since we've discussed anger/rage, isolation and criminality, how about the Catholic Church? I had no place to put my*

anger since I could not talk about my family, but the Catholic Church
was available. I come from a good Irish Catholic family so of course I
was an altar boy. So when the scandal broke in 2002, I was horrified
just like everybody else, but since I had not remembered my abuse,
that was that.

However, once I remembered, things changed. I now had a place
to dump my anger and I was looking for some comrades-in-arms, so I
decided to attend one of those masses of reconciliation that Cardinal
O'Malley was giving. (It just so happened to be the church where my
wife and I were married. It was also the last time we were in a Catholic Church). I was looking for a group of survivors that I could belong
to and God only knows what else I was seeking. Anyway, I met some
SNAP members picketing outside and I had a conversation with an
ex-seminarian who had been abused. He asked if I was sure I wanted
to go inside and of course I thought I was.

My opinion: It was a dog and pony show and I left half-way
through the mass. I stepped outside and this woman came up to me.
She asked if I was Don. I said, "Yes, how did you know?" She said she
was told to watch for me. I guess the ex-seminarian was right: I should
not have gone in and I needed some talking down. We talked for a
while and I thought I was okay, but walking back to the car I could
hear the Cardinal's voice. I had this urge to run in there and just
punch him. That damned rage sprang up again, but I did not act on
the rage – I just went home.

Me: How is your rage now?

Don: Much better.

Me: What has helped decrease that rage and anger?

Don: I now know where the anger is coming from.

Me: Clarity?

*Don: Yes, and the breakdown of the isolation. I was in a therapeutic
group for male survivors at THP for about twenty-four weeks and a
few individual sessions with Maddie.*

Me: How did you find out about THP?

Don: Some sort of divine intervention. I was on my way to see a client and I saw an ad on the train. When I got to my client's apartment, the first thing I saw was a brochure for the THP fundraiser which my client's girlfriend was participating in. Twice in ten minutes seeing THP? I paid attention. So I called and asked to be in a men's group. One formed about eight months later and I was in. Be careful what you ask for!

I can't begin to tell you how painful it was to go through that group, especially the first twelve weeks. It was awful. Just plain fucking awful. It sucked. Every Monday night when I left, I would walk around the local baseball field two or three times just to calm down and to feel safe enough to drive home.

Me: Why was it so awful?

Don: Because all of this stuff was coming up. All of this stuff was coming out.

(Long pause)

Sometimes it's really tough to face reality. Individual therapy is one thing, but to be in a room with other men and talking about it and they're talking about it: Ouch! It's not just talking, it's also the feeling it. I did everything in my power to stay numb as long as I could, and I was good at it, ya know? It felt like all of a sudden the walls were coming down. It was like, "Holy fuck, HELP!!!"

The worst night was when one guy (who is now a friend of mine) saw a TV show about predators and how their minds worked (or didn't work) for about half an hour, which seemed like three hours to me. The anxiety was incredible. I kept wringing my hands and I was disassociating like crazy. I did not care in the least about learning about the mind of a pedophile. I felt extremely unsafe, but I stuck it out.

Another time, early on in the group process, maybe the second or third week, we went around the group, and each man was to give two *or three sentences about the actual abuse. I got as far as, "This guy had his forearm across my neck," and I lost it. I dropped my clipboard on the floor and I guess I was disassociating big time and trying to hold it all together, i.e., not becoming psychotic. I just couldn't talk about it. The exercise stopped, everybody else had to put down their clipboards, and we did some breathing exercises instead. I felt bad that I "disrupted" the group!*

Those sorts of things happened, but I was able to sit through the pain and anxiety, and that was real good, ya know? I stuck it out and came out the other end a new and improved man. "It ain't easy" but it was worth it. I have a couple of friends from that group that I still have contact with.

Me: What else has helped you in the healing process?

Don: The most important thing to me is talking to other survivors; it cuts down the isolation.

Me: You said earlier the isolation is the hardest part.

Don: Yeah. Isolation is the worst because while in isolation, there is no place to go with any of this stuff. I've been fortunate with some luck and a whole lotta work. I am in contact with other male survivors. I mentioned earlier that I have a couple of friends from my therapy group. I am now in a male survivor peer led group; we meet every other week. Most weeks there are between five and seven of us. It's just knowing that twice a month I will be under the same roof as other survivors. We are all there for the same reason.

Me: I would love to spread this book and its messages if that is possible. What would you like people to know about this crime? About you? About how we can attempt to change this?"

Don: Okay... ummm...it's important to know that it is a crime. That's...ya know...ummm... it's not about sex... it's about power.

(Long pause)

It's very violent. You can't describe the violence. It's just...it's overwhelming how violent it is. To be held down and raped...I incor-

porated that into my personal life and I held myself down, or I just allowed my perpetrator's forearm to stay on my neck and his fingers up my ass; the whole thing. That stayed with me my whole life and I didn't even know it. It is beyond mind boggling to me that at fifty-eight years old, I wake up and say, "Wow! This happened to me. My whole fucking life is gone. This is why I never finished college. This is why I'm an alcoholic. This is why I've had some sexual problems. This is why I've had depression. This is why, this is why, this is why."

The toughest part for me is being able to accept that it did indeed happen and that is has affected every area of my life. It was the most important event in my life and I could not even fight it until I was in my mid-fifties because I didn't know it happened. Also, I am very lucky. I may have remembered late in life, but I did in fact remember and I have gotten a lot of help. I have met some very remarkable male and female survivors.

So when people want to know about these repressed memories, they are real. They are not fake or manufactured. I have nothing to gain from this. Nothing. Nothing at all. I am not suing anybody. Male and female survivors don't come forward for attention (far from it) or money; they come forward to get validation of the fact it did happen. I think that is what is important to me – validation and help (both giving and receiving) from others. I can't get that from my perpetrator.

Me: It is mind boggling to me that you did not remember being sexually abused until you were in your mid-fifties.

Don: It truly is mind boggling that it took half a century for me to remember, and it's not just the mind; it's the body. The body remembers. I mean touch to me can be…I cringe sometimes when I get touched. I sometimes associate touch with pain, even after all these years. No matter how much I know in my head, it's still here in my body as well. I sometimes wonder how many men and women have died in their forties, fifties, and sixties and never even knew they were abused, or how many knew they were abused and never told anyone.

Me: I'd say more than we can imagine.

Don: People need that information. You asked what I should tell people. Talk about it and then talk about it some more. Bring it out. This is what happens to kids. This is how it can affect the rest of their lives. But always know that it doesn't have to.

It's pretty much impossible to describe the pain. It's like everything is just pressed on top, being pinned down and you can't do anything about it. You don't have any words to explain it. All this stuff comes closing in and that's how I stayed for all those decades.

It is mandatory that I remember that I am not a victim. I was victimized, and every time I do any sort of self-destructive behavior, I am giving more power to my uncle. Likewise, any time I do the next right thing, I am taking back my power. I'm going to the THP fundraiser this weekend. Even coming here to your apartment – it's all good because I'm taking my power back.

Me: How are you doing? Are you okay?

Don: Yeah.

Me: I truly believe in healing. People really do get better. If they didn't then I wouldn't be doing this. Given that healing does exist and it is real, I have still seen many people blame themselves. Most, if not all the survivors I've met through THP and in my personal life, to various degrees have blamed themselves. It is my opinion that when they stop blaming themselves, then their whole world changes. Do you agree?

Don: Yes.

Me: How can people stop the self blame and free up the pressure in their bodies and minds for themselves?

Don: Mentally, spiritually, and physically: all three of them. I was full of shame. Just full of it. Even though I didn't do anything, I still have shame. That shame has been decreased a lot, but shame and anxiety are still there. I still can get nervous around sex or talking about sex. I can get very nervous. Not all the time, but sometimes. The guilt and the shame…it's crazy. There is nothing I could have done about the abuse. I was victimized. The guy was around thirty and I was four; it was not a fair fight. God only knows what happened after that but anyway…

So the healing happens by talking about it. Taking care of the body is a great help also. Primal therapy was all about my body. It was about feeling and then releasing some body pain. I also go to a men's retreat twice a year where there is a sweat lodge, drumming, dance, and also some ritual work. It's all from the neck down – just let 'er rip. That has helped release my body and put a smile on my face.

Me: What else puts a smile on your face?

Don: *Holding my wife's hand. That's the whole thing. I'll never forget that night. Pretty fucked up, isn't it?*

Me: It is. I mean…

Don: *That's negative. That's the way it was. It's changed.*

Me: It's real.

Don: *It's real.*

Me: This crime transcends gender, age, ethnicity, religion, socio-economic status, sexual orientation, anything. As you already said, it's an act of violence. I also think it's an act of evil.

Don: *It is evil and it is so fucking violent. The violence of my rape(s) was incredible. Through primal therapy, I remembered the sounds my uncle was making during the assault – really awful violent noises that sounded almost inhuman. There was tons of pain there. He did not sound like he was having a good time at all.*

You know what else has helped? I went on the Oprah show and I went there with 199 other male survivors to put my face to this thing. This old guy with the white moustache – it happened to him. That was me taking some more of my power back.

Me: As you mentioned earlier, you have had quite a bit of anger toward the Catholic Church. Do you believe in God?

Don: *Absolutely, but not the Catholic God of my youth.*

Me: So do I. I believe God is begging us to give our pain away.

Don: *Oh yeah, I get that. I fully get that. That's what happened to me a few weeks ago. I sat up and realized I'm keeping this pain* *and that's not good. That's me being self-destructive. I gotta get rid of this shit, this anger, this pain, and that's what I am doing. That's part of what I am doing here right now. I may be a bit anxious for the next day or two, but after that, it's all good. I will have dumped some more shit. Name it, claim it, and dump it.*

Me: And you will continue to.

Don: Yes. My personal opinion is true healing happens from the neck down. The head is good, and then you bring it on down to the gut. My first experience with that was thinking about alcoholism. I remember the morning clear as a bell. I knew in my gut that the next drink was going to kill me. I just knew, and I still know it, and that was over thirty years ago. It wasn't until it was in my gut and heart that I was able to act on it. Once it gets into my gut, heart, and soul, it is real. The gut knows. The heart knows. God knows. We are all part of that. So yeah, I believe the spiritual healing has to happen. It is happening and you are part of the whole process.

Me: Me?

Don: Yeah, you.

Me: Thank you.

Don: Maddie said something that has always stuck with me. I asked her, "How can you work with survivors of childhood sexual abuse? Isn't it depressing?" She said it isn't depressing at all. She said it's hopeful because she sees people getting better.

Me: I totally agree. I see people getting better and I see such strength in some people. You inspire me to keep doing. This is not the easiest job. But when I hear things like I'm hearing today and I see people like you, Jim, and all of the others I've come across, I get inspired. It's people like you that inspire me. You really do. And Maddie is right. She's absolutely right. I can't speak for her, but I'll speak for myself. Have there been moments of depression? Of course. But the things that we see from people like you are one of the greatest gifts in the world: To see a person change and get better.

So I'll leave it with you. Is there anything else you would like to say? Is there one last final statement you would like to share with people?

Don: *If it happened to somebody or they suspected it did happen, even if they vaguely thought it occurred, that means it probably did. Go see a professional and get some help. I'm glad I came here today.*
Me: I'm glad you did too. How do you feel?
Don: *Tired, but good.*

    Don and I continued to talk about his plans for self-care that afternoon, sports, and religion. We both thanked each other and then he left my apartment. Later in the day I got a phone call from a woman informing me I did not get a job I had been waiting three months to get. But I wasn't even upset. The fact that I didn't get the job was the last thing on my mind given what Don had just shared with me. My family was sad for me because they knew how excited I was for the job. But I said to everyone, "It's all good. You have no idea what I just heard. Trust me, I'm good. There are more important things in life than getting that job."

    The next day I flew to Myrtle Beach to vacation with some of my family. On the balcony overlooking the ocean with a mimosa in hand, I sent an email to Don to see how he was doing. I wanted to make sure he was okay. I wrote:

Hey Don,

It was a pleasure to meet you yesterday. How was the rest of your night? How are you doing today? I just wanted to check in and make sure you are doing well.

-Bobby

Don responded:

Bobby,

    Thanks for checking in. I had some anxiety while at your place, thus some excess chatter. I was a little charged up later that day and up into the night, but the anxiety was miniscule compared to what I felt after each group at THP, ergo, I have made much progress. Because I get anxiety, I often omit some important information when talking, and yesterday was no different. So let me put in a few important things regarding my recovery (if any of this is redundant, I apologize).

1) *I am now able to distinguish between feeling uncomfortable vs. unsafe (extremely important).*

2) *My body remembered the pain. Therapeutic bodywork has helped me immensely. I can remember the exact moment during a massage when a male therapist was touching my stomach and I felt totally relaxed. That was a great "aha" moment.*

3) *The abuse was not my fault.*

4) *It is now okay for me to seek and enjoy pleasure.*

5) *Self-care – when in doubt, do the next right thing.*

6) *Redirection. Last week I was listening to a radio show about the constitutionality of strip-searching. I became very uneasy when I heard some of the graphic talk. I shut off the radio and began to get physically busy i.e., wash sheets, walk dog, clean kitchen, and I was fine. I have knowledge and tools I did not previously have, and I can, and so, use them.*

7) *Reaching out to others.*

8) *Prayer.*

9) *Telephoning peers in recovery.*

10) *Deep breathing.*

11) *Walking.*

12) *Exercise.*

13) *Credit myself when I utilize self-care and gratitude.*

14) *Being open for other survivors when they need an ear or anything i.e., co-creating, utilizing, and appreciating a healing community.*

Again, many thanks for giving me the opportunity to tell my story. I know from my alcoholic recovery, each time I tell my abuse story, it will become easier. And each time I tell the story, part of that story physically leaves my body. Amen to that.

It was also fantastic that we were able to have a great discussion on spirituality. You are an easy man to both talk to and listen to. Love your energy, spirit, and enthusiasm. Keep rockin'.

AND For the first time in my life, because you shared your tattoos and the spiritual reasons for getting them, I am actually thinking about getting one. It will be a triangle inside a circle which is the AA symbol. It will be cool to honor the symbol of the beginning of my spiritual life and connection to a Higher Power (funny, I have been coming across a lot of Jesus and his teaching lately, including our talk yesterday). Etching the symbol into my skin will be a powerful statement.

I hope and look forward to our paths crossing again (soon).
Until then, Be Well and Be Blessed!!!
Don

Don and I kept in touch. We continued to discuss his story and life in general. We also worked on the editing process together. Throughout this process, Don shared this:

Don: One more very important thing: Since we last talked, I took an all day seminar with an aikido (type of martial art). It was amazing and freeing. The instructor pinned me down just like my uncle, including the forearm on my neck, and I was able to throw him off! For real! Boy did that feel good and have I felt a little lighter since. I was taught how to, and I actually did, throw the fucker off.

Two strangers thirty-five years apart first met at an apartment to share a story. That morning turned out to be the beginning of a bond between

Don and me. Don is a good man, and I'm thankful our paths have crossed. I enjoyed meeting Don, and I admire him for the fact that he really wants to make a difference in other people's lives. He constantly thanked me for giving him the opportunity to share his story, but he always talks about how he hopes it connects to just one person. It's worth it if one person gains something from his story.

Don confided in me that he feels he did not spend most of his life living up to his full potential. He says the root cause of his problems throughout his life was the sexual abuse inflicted upon him by his uncle during his childhood. But now he knows the abuse happened and he knows why he had so many problems. Don has grown and continues down a healing path, and he told me he is looking forward to the future. Don said to me that morning, ***"I have a lot of life left in me. A lot of life."***

Chapter 17

CHRIS

———

"And then you realize that this clearly is not about me. This cannot be about my character. There are thirty men in this room of all different sorts coming from all different walks of life who had this singular experience, and because of this have this very clear set of results and symptoms in their life. You begin to see that this cannot be just me. The power of that is really helpful in removing some of the shame and stepping into one's power."

Chris was the second person with whom Jim connected me. He and I spoke on the phone and discussed my ideas for the book. Chris decided that he wanted to contribute, so I invited him over to my apartment for dinner and some wine. We talked about THP, sexual violence, music, basketball, his ambition to finish school, and career possibilities. After hanging out with Chris for about two hours, I could tell that he is a very intelligent, caring, empathetic, and thoughtful human being. He's a great guy who truly cares and contemplates the suffering of others.

The night Chris and I had dinner was the first time we ever met. Just as what happened with Don, neither one of us knew what would come out or what to expect. This is Chris' story:

Chris: This happened when I was either nine or ten. There was a place that my family would go to every summer. It was a family camp in New Hampshire, which was a great place. You would see the same families there every single year, and you would get to know these people. You would grow a year older, but it was nice to reconnect with folks and be a part of the sense of community that was there.

You stayed in these log cabin sorts of things. It was very rustic. Meals were eaten together in a very kind of communal way. I think I've probably visited there over the course of maybe seven or eight years. I would go every summer and I have very fond memories about going there. This family camp ended up being the location where the abuse took place. It was the last year I went there.

One of the things that happens at this camp is there are separate activities for kids. They have counselors, but the counselors often varied every summer. In 1990 or 1991, I met one of the counselors named Marcelo. I was nine or ten. He spoke Spanish, although I'm not sure which country he came from. He was a very, very, charismatic fellow. He was well-liked by kids, and he just had a really good way with people.

I've been dealing with the abuse and looking at it in a very different way and taking it a lot more seriously in terms of the impact it's had on my life. I try to recall. I try to go back over the course of the week. I was there for about a week. I try to recall different feelings I had when I was there. I try to recall different visual experiences I can remember about places I was, or times I was with this guy. I'm definitely remembering more.

It's never been something that I haven't known happened to me. I was always aware that "it" happened. I think it's my understanding of what "it" is that's changed a lot. Trying to understand what exactly it is that's going on is difficult when you're nine or ten. You don't have the same sense, obviously, as if you were older or had more context and understanding.

The counselors met all of the kids on the first day of camp. Marcelo took a particular liking to me. He befriended me. My parents divorced just prior so I was just there with my dad. In the past both my mom and dad would go along with my sister who is three and half years younger than me. But this was the first time I went with just one parent. It was just my dad and I. So pretty much on day one he befriended me, and then abuse occurred over the course of a week. There were three different times when some form of abuse was taking place, although I think there were more.

I can't quite remember everything, but I do have some specific memories. It's hard to chronologically order it in time, but looking back at it now, he was grooming me. I can remember specific things. He would often try to get me to go off and do things just with him. One time I remember we walked right across the island after dinner, which takes about thirty minutes. It was dark. We went to some big rock and we were talking.

All of the times I was with him, there was a part of me that did not want to be there. I was trying to think of a way to not be in the situation. That's the most innocuous memory I have. It was mostly just walking, and then we ended up at some rock looking out over the water. It was dark or dusk. I can't remember if anything physical happened then.

I have another memory where we were up in the game room of this place. There was a foosball table and other games, but it was private. We were playing a game together and he set the rules for the game. If he wins the game something happens, and if I win the game something happens. And both of the things that happened were not things that I wanted to happen. It was sort of like, if he wins something happens. If

I win, he teaches me how to french kiss. That was my prize to win the game.

Me: The prize of winning the game was to learn how to french kiss?

Chris: Yeah. That was either if I won or he won. I remember feeling that it didn't really matter who won the game and that it was essentially irrelevant. I remember us kissing. I remember his tongue in my mouth...

Unpleasant...

(Pause)

There are different ways in which that week has impacted my life since, but ways which are much clearer are being with someone sexually now. I guess I could talk about that later.

The last memory I have involves the most overt, physical, sexual abuse. One night he invited me back to his dorm where he stayed. We went into his room and he locked the door. He then showed me some pictures of little boys. He showed me pictures of his "friends". That's what he called them.

Me: What was it?

Chris: Pictures. Pictures of him and other kids, around the same age mostly. Some were younger and some were older. He had A LOT of pictures. There were A LOT of pictures. There were a lot of different kids. His room had a desk with a little computer on it and there was a light. And his bed was in the back of the room. He had a guitar as well.

More physical stuff happened over time. At first it was kissing. He then fondled me. He put his hands on my ass. He moved my hands to different places on him, so I would be touching him. We did this while we were standing up. He also asked if I could get an erection. I said "no", which was not true. And then three or four minutes later afterward he was touching me, or I was touching him, and I did have an erection. He playfully joked and said, "Oh, look you can. You lied to me."

So we were standing up at first, doing these things. Eventually we end up lying down on his bed, and it was more or less of the same. He either guided me with his hands or just verbally told me what he wanted me to be doing. I was touching his back. I was touching his butt. I was basically fondling him, and there was kissing that went on as well.

(Long pause)

I think I had most of a visceral memory of that, because it sort of felt like a foreign object in my mouth. It was almost like a slug, sort of like a slimy forceful something, which is not myself. I told one person about this when I was fifteen. It was my closest friend. I didn't end up telling my parents until I was seventeen.

Me: How did they respond?

Chris: *They both felt really bad. My mom felt more visibly bad. I think it was harder for her to process because everyone thought this place was a wonderful safe family place. And my mom wasn't there that year.*

Me: Some people tend to think, "No one thinks that's gonna happen at a place like this."

Chris: *Exactly. I hadn't spoken about it. I think parents have this underlying belief that if something is wrong with their kid, their kid is going to tell them if something bad happened. They think their kid will somehow communicate it to them. And I've subsequently found out that is the exception. That is by far the exception. Most people that this happens to do not tell anyone for a very long time.*

My parents were very upset. They were more upset over it than I was. The way that I dealt with it was to separate myself from it a bit. I remember during it where I understood, or felt like I understood what he wanted. And so I would sort of give him enough, but not too much, and then try to find my way out of situations with him. That was my attempt to control what was going on. And for a really long time, even later, that's how I thought about it. There was this really bad thing that happened to me, but it never escalated to the point where I was physically forced.

I can understand now intellectually that something cannot be physically forced, and yet it's still a tremendous act of force and a tremendous act of power. Whatever belief I had about control in that situation was just sort of my own attempt to believe I had some power in the situation when I really didn't. There's also a difference between having an intellectual understanding of that being true, and really believing and fully knowing that's true.

I can still tell there is a disconnect. Some part of me still wants to believe, or can't let go of the fact that I still had some control over what was happening. My sense is, as I continue on and come to terms with it through-out the healing process, that there will be more of a connection. I'll be able to connect more to the realization that I really didn't have much or any control at all. But it's helpful to be savvy and say that there's that discrepancy.

So my parents were upset. My mom actually ended up calling the camp. She wanted justice. She said, "If this guy is still there, why wasn't there oversight! Do you know where this guy is?" She ended up talking with someone there. They said they kept really shoddy records. People would come for a year and disappear, and they have no idea where they went. So they had no idea where Marcelo was. But the guy said that he was going to call back and talk to me, basically to apolo-gize to me, which never ended up happening.

Me: Who did he say that to?

Chris: To my mom.

Me: He said he was gonna apologize to you?

Chris: The person that she talked to. This wasn't the abuser. This was the guy running the camp.

Me: So he admitted his employee's guilt?

Chris: I don't know. This was now seven or eight years later. So the guy might not have been there back then. He might not have been

*there earlier. He might have been, but I'm not sure. I don't know.
I think from hearing my mom, my sense is that he felt like it was
probably true. Why would a mom randomly call up and accuse?*

Me: It fascinates me because I can't imagine a human being saying to
someone's mother, "I am going to apologize to your son" and then not
apologize. That is mind blowing to me. To me, you either do something or
you don't. None of this kind of in between...

*Chris: Yeah. I mean it's a hard thing for someone to deal with. I
don't mean to excuse the guy running the camp, but I think this
stuff is just tough to begin with. People just don't know how to deal
with this stuff, even people who probably have good intentions. It's
just hard. I sure wish the guy called back and apologized to me in
whatever way he could, even if he wasn't there when it happened. It
would have been nice if he had stepped up and done it. I would have
appreciated it.*

*I want to get back to where I was trying to go, which is the second
part of that story when I was with this guy Marcelo in his room. I
want to say it was twenty minutes, but I don't really know. My dad,
who was there during that weekend, remembers seeing Marcelo and
I standing in a field somewhere together, and then walking off somewhere. My dad remembers that something was not quite right about
the energy. Something just felt not quite right. And so he started walking and trying to figure out where we went.*

*I don't remember any of this, but he found Marcelo and I walking
out of Marcelo's room. His room was where the staff stays, sort of like
a big dormitory. There was a first and second floor. So we came out
of the second floor and walked down the stairwell to the first floor.
My dad says that he encountered Marcelo and I walking down the
stairs together. He confronted Marcelo saying, "Whoa! What were
you guys doing!" I guess Marcelo said something like, "Oh, I was
teaching Chris music. I was teaching him how to play the guitar." My
dad said he looked directly at me, and he was trying to get a sense of
where I was or gauge something about where I was. He said I didn't*

portray any emotion. I gave him no reason to think that something was happening that shouldn't have been happening. And that was that.

So that's another interesting piece about the whole story. This is all happening and my dad is there. My dad gets this far as to actually getting there thirty seconds or a minute after the abuse is happening, getting right up to the point of almost figuring out and actually seeing what was happening, and yet not quite making the final jump. So that is interesting.

As I've read a lot more and understood a lot more about abuse in the past couple of years, I've learned that abuse often happens, or kids get chosen, in families where there isn't a lot of support or there's a lot of turmoil at home. So I think about that. I think about if my dad were a different sort of dad, or if he were a different sort of way, maybe I wouldn't have been selected. Or maybe he could have actually stopped that situation or actually confronted it there.

Me: Maybe.

Chris: Maybe.

Me: Maybe not.

Chris: Maybe not.

Me: Maybe you were stone cold just to survive.

Chris: Sure.

Me: It could have been out of fear or out of shock. And you did what you had to do at the time to survive out of fear of the unknown.

Chris: For sure… yeah…that's my way of understanding why I didn't portray any emotion. It didn't feel safe for me to do that. It must not have.

Another overriding feeling I have about that week is that notion of secrecy, or that notion of hiding. My dad told another story about my attempts to indirectly communicate. I guess he remembered a story where I told him something like, "I could run really fast if I needed to." I made that kind of comment, which I think was an indirect way of communicating. I don't know. There's ways to read into something, but that feels to me like a significant story, not really knowing how to speak about this thing that was happening to me.

These are the three memories I have directly. Two of them involved physical stuff, but one more dramatically so. My sense is over the course of a weekend, there was in particular more kissing that went on, and I know I had a lot more interactions with Marcelo. I wonder too, because of course with this stuff, there's often memory loss and repression. And so I think maybe there's something else. Maybe there's more I'm not remembering. If there was, I'd like to remember it. But there might not be.

My overall feeling about the weekend is that somehow while I was being really strongly pressed upon, a part of me was keeping enough control, keeping enough of my voice. I feel like I didn't break. My feeling is that, if there had been overt force, I wouldn't have kept that feeling. I would have felt that breaking point, but instead I just sort of left with a deep wounding. It was just a deep wounding.

Me: What do you mean by a "deep wounding"?

Chris: I'm just trying to clearly articulate what I mean by it.

Me: I ask because there is this notion of coercion. Mental coercion combined with fear of the unknown or fear of worse can be terrifying and crippling. Do you think that played a role?

Chris: Yeah for sure. When I think about the week, I think about the experience of feeling like someone was pressing upon me. It's like the force of him or something. But it's interesting because there was never a point when he held my hands, but yet I still have this very strong sense of this force that was exerted. So yeah, the threat of force, or the unknowing of it, or the fact that it's mental or emotional coercion, or even the sense that I felt like I had to give him something. If I didn't give him anything, then the physical force would come into play.

Me: That's what I'm getting at.

Chris: Yeah.

Me: What would happen if you didn't? Perpetrators will often use as much physical force as necessary. That's just what I've learned in my experiences.

Chris: *That makes sense.*

Me: So many people who have these experiences somehow think that they "gave in". They think that it wasn't against their will because they "consented" to it. But assent is different than consent.

Chris: *Yeah. Definitely.*

Me: Ya know what I mean? And especially at your age. Especially as a child.

Chris: *Exactly. That's the primary thing. When you have an adult and a child, and there's something sexual involved, the details almost don't matter. By definition, the ages and the activity mean that there's force. It means that there's not consent.*

It's funny. Even when I talk about the force or whatever, I think a lot of times about the impacts it has on you. It manifests in many different ways. I know there's a lot of research and work recently on how it impacts the body. I can still feel the force in my chest, almost like a clamping down or something. I'm thirty now, and so it's been over twenty years since the abuse, and it's just been in the past two years that I've really come to understand its impact. But when I look back at the past twenty years, there's been a great deal of suffering in my life. I've dealt with depression almost endlessly since then.

And the parts of my life or the moments in my life that I feel like I'm struggling the most, either in a depression, or a lot of times when it will come up is when there will be a fear or a mistrust. That can be when I'm in a relationship with another, or going after something in the world that I want. I'll disengage instead of engaging. And very often what comes from that is this sort of, almost clamping down in my chest. Whatever force that was exerted on me then or whatever sort of structure I had to create within myself was a protective shield. It was something that I can still viscerally connect to. When I'm speaking right now I can connect to it right now, right in my chest.

I compare my story to other stories. I had this brief contact for a week with no clear physical impact, but I still carry the remnants of it in my chest twenty years later. The power of that experience is pretty profound...

(Long pause)

Me: How are you doing?

Chris: *I'm okay. Maybe one of the most useful things I've found in the past couple of years is connecting with the feelings I have about this. It's very difficult. There's another piece to it which is rising to the surface. Just speaking about it creates space for growth. There is something to speaking. When I connect to the feelings and speak about it, I tap into a part of myself which doesn't often get tapped into. It feels really good and important to tap into. And so I'm okay.*

Me: What do you mean by that?

Chris: *Another clear result I can see from abuse is that I ended up disconnecting from my feelings a lot. In some ways that's part of what depression is: You're not able to access certain feelings. You restrict what you're able to experience, and as you restrict negative feelings, that makes it impossible for you to feel the corollary positive feelings. Part of my healing has been finding ways to reconnect with what I feel. When I speak about stuff like this and share my story, there's a clear connection to those feelings. And just by experiencing those feelings, relating to them, speaking them out loud, there's just something healing about it.*

Me: The abuse has clearly affected your life negatively. The depression may have been caused by that. Has the abuse and the depression kept you or deterred you from doing things that you love, such as playing the piano like you talked about earlier?

Chris: *No. I've played soccer since a young age as well. I find areas of refuge essentially. For me, playing soccer, being out in the field, and using my body is something I love. I look back on the past twenty years and realize time has been spent playing on the soccer field, being in connection with others, and building a skill. I have incredibly fond memories of that. I have a great love of playing and for using my body in athletics. I've certainly found ways to connect with things that I enjoy.*

As I've done more healing and looking at this more, it opens up more space. There's less fear. There's less anxiety. There's certainly more of a willingness to trust in the world. And the more I do that, the more I'm able to engage more with the world and actively pursue more things. I'm going back to school to finish my B.A. finally.

I went to college out of high school and I was struggling horribly with depression. Doing school work felt almost meaningless. I was like "why?" There was such heaviness in my heart. There was so much suffering in my life that completing an assignment was irrelevant. It was nothing. So the fact that I'm actively now back in school is a good thing. The experience of being in school now is just so dramatically different from when it was when I was nineteen and twenty. And so to me that's a testament to the fact that there have been things in me that I've been changing, shifting, growing, and healing, and I can feel it. I experience the world in a different way now.

I have dealt with depression for twenty years and still do, but there were still times that I could find joy in life. But in particular, I remember when I first started recognizing two years ago that the abuse had the impact it had. It was in some ways almost like a relief. It was like, "Now I have a way to understand all the suffering I've experienced in my life." Because before it I thought, "I feel terrible. I don't want to be awake. I don't know why." It just felt like this horrible… it almost felt worse when I couldn't find a direct reason or cause. So having the recognition of, "Wait a second, this thing that happened to me", was very powerful and profound. I'm willing to delve into it more, and then maybe this is going to be a key to unlock what so much of my struggle has been.

I have spoken with a number of guys who have dealt with abuse. It's always interesting to hear what in their life prompts all of a sudden, either remembering the abuse or realizing its impact. I don't have kids myself, but a number of guys talk about once their kid hits a certain age, the age that they were abused, all of a sudden flashbacks start coming back and they just kind of get hit with it.

For me, it happened in March two years ago. I had a really important relationship in my life with this girl. We had a very ambiguous relationship. There were clearly romantic elements. We both cared about one another a great deal. That relationship ended. I was fine for a couple of weeks, and then all of a sudden I kind of fell apart. After those couple of weeks, after we broke up and I told her I couldn't see her, I then went into a two week period where something broke inside of me. Something just broke.

I've experienced depression, and sometimes very debilitating depression, but what I experienced over those two weeks was unlike anything I had previously experienced, meaning the extent of the pain. I would sob for hours. I remember the sun would go down and I would be on my hands and knees just sobbing.

I had thought about suicide before, but during those two weeks was the first time I really thought, "Wait a second. If I keep feeling like this, I cannot be alive anymore." That seemed to start something for me. I think the trigger was ending this relationship. I had known this girl for five or six years. Our relationship was really important. I was seen by her in a way I haven't been by someone else. Ending that relationship kind of broke something in me, like something I'd been holding onto. She even talked about it. She felt like whatever I was experiencing and dealing with wasn't really about her. At the time I was angry at her for saying that, but I think she was quite right. Whatever broke in me was the accumulation of pain I've been storing literally in my body, which I couldn't hold anymore, or which my body just decided to let go of. I see that as marking the past couple of years, which have been very different for me.

I've been in therapy before when I was younger, in particular for stuff like depression. I'm currently seeing a therapist who I have a great deal of respect for in so many ways. I actually told previous therapists about the abuse. There was one guy who took me seriously, but who I stopped seeing after two or three times after I told him. This was still after I felt like the abuse wasn't that big of a deal. There were a couple of other therapists who I had told about the abuse, but they didn't seem to think it was a big deal.

Me: They didn't think it was a big deal?

Chris: No.

Me: What did they think?

Chris: I don't know. As I've read more too, in particular for me who has dealt with abuse, it's actually just in the past ten or twenty years when therapists even recognized how widespread abuse in male victims was. In the past they didn't know the extent of it. Now some believe there are one in six. In the past they probably would have guessed one in a hundred or one in a thousand or something. So it's a very recent thing, and I think a lot of therapists weren't trained. They didn't know how to deal with it, and that's changing a lot. But yeah, in another way I hear your question. How much training do you need to not recognize...

Me: In my humble opinion, you don't need to be a brain surgeon to figure that one out. That's just me.

Chris: Yeah for sure. For the past two years I've been seeing my therapist on a weekly basis. I've done a lot of work with her and that's been incredibly helpful. Additionally, a year and a half ago, I met and began a romantic relationship with a tremendously kind and empathic girl. Through being vulnerable with her, and through having her sit with me, even when I put up walls as I so often do in relationships with other people, I've grown a lot. She's helped me to recognize the impact of the abuse in my life. And just the amount of patience, love, and compassion she's shown me. My willingness to stay open and vulnerable with her has been important, as historically it had been very difficult for me.

So yeah, those are probably the three biggest things: The initial two week period of deep suffering and thoughts of suicide, then becom-

ing involved with a relationship with this therapist who has been incredibly helpful, and then my romantic relationship with this girl. There's been a lot of other stuff too.

I mentioned earlier to you as well that I've always done a lot of self-examining, and there's always irony, right? Some might argue I've done self-examining because I knew there was something that was there to be looked for. Some of it might have just been part of my makeup, regardless of whether I've been abused or not. I'm just interested in certain aspects of the human experience. But it's funny to think that I'm so interested in self-examining, yet it took me a long time to really understand the impact of the abuse.

There are other things I've done which have been very helpful for me in my healing process. I found that yoga was really good for me. We talked a little bit about the importance of how the abuse can lodge itself in your body. So it can be helpful to recognize that some of the thoughts and beliefs you have about yourself are a bit distorted, or incredibly distorted. That's a nice way to approach or understand. There is something beyond cognitive insight. Your body remembers things, and there's a way you can work with your body, so yoga did that for me. It was a really powerful way of reconnecting with my body.

Me: Did it help reconnecting with your feelings as well that you talked about earlier?

Chris: Yeah. I think so. I think all of it is connected really. Feelings can be stored in your body. I know for a lot of people, especially some guys who do yoga, it can be quite frightening because they'll reconnect with their body and then they'll have a flood of feelings or a flood of emotions which will rise up as well. I haven't had as many experiences like that which are so dramatic of feelings, but just as a general sense of reconnecting with myself and who I am and what my boundaries are; it's been very helpful.

I actually found meditation really helpful. That's a different approach. There's also cognitive behavioral therapy, which is retrain-

ing one's thinking. You question assumptions about the world, or others, or one's self which might not be accurate. For me, meditation does that in a very similar way where if you sit with yourself, you start to notice things. You start to notice patterns that your mind has, or messages you repeat to yourself, or things will just rise up to consciousness. So I find that to be really useful. Apart from just being calming, it's been helpful in finding a different knowledge about myself.

By far the most important thing is just the importance of connecting with others. I think that is the biggest thing. I think the saddest result of abuse is how restricted one's experience ends up being, how much one withdraws, protects one's self, and isolates one's self. That is what depression is. You restrict your experience so much that of course it feels terrible. You're not willing to engage. Making meaningful connections with others is sort of the meat of what being human is. I don't think people seek that out when their trust is destroyed. You find every reason to not connect. You see the potential for someone hurting you, or someone judging you, or someone finding fault in everything, so it keeps you from engaging.

Connecting with others, whether it's in a relationship like I talked about with my girlfriend, or being a part of this men's group for abuse survivors, is really helpful. And these weekends of recovery with male survivors...I mean Jesus Christ... those things are incredibly powerful. God...

Me: How are they helpful and how are they so powerful?

Chris: I went to one last year in California, and the first thing I think that you notice is there's such a feeling of being understood without words. There's a feeling of camaraderie. It's almost like you just recognize in the other that there's been this important shared experience. There's this feeling of safety, or brotherhood, or connection. The weekend takes place over three days. The amount of vulnerability that's expressed and the amount of safety you feel on the first day is just...it's just...I have not experienced it in relationships

I've had with people that have lasted over a decade. You have this
shared experience that's so powerful that it just creates this bond.

Me: Is there a feeling of love?

Chris: Yeah. For sure.

Me: Is it more powerful than someone you've known for many years?

Chris: Yeah.

Me: Wow…That is powerful.

Chris: Yeah. And that's another thing. Everyone shares a different
story, but somehow there's a kernel of truth within each story that
people just connect around. There's a two hour segment where we
broke up into small groups, and we were basically sharing our story
with one another. I was just in tears the entire time hearing these
other men speak about what happened to them. It was almost like
when they were speaking part of myself was responding. It's like they
were speaking my words. I felt like they were speaking to some part of
me. There was this resonance.

   There was a guy there who was in his forties, and he was very
cut off from himself. It was just clear. He had very little affect. He
hit a point that reminded me of a year earlier. Something just broke
in him. I sat there while something in this guy broke. He went from
someone who was essentially sitting there robotically to wailing and
screaming. It was like, "Are you there? Are you there?" to this out-
pouring of emotion. They were two opposite extremes. It was hard to
breathe. So connecting with other survivors and sharing one's own
story is very important and powerful. That first weekend was very
powerful.

Me: Is there anything else that you wanna say? Anything else you wanna
talk about? Anything else you want people to know?

Chris: I guess the two things that seem the most important are there
are communities now. There is support. People will hear you. There
are ways to connect and find community, and no matter how much
you think what occurred to you is unspeakable, or if you feel this
speaks to your character, or how much shame or guilt you feel about

it, know that there is someone who will sit with you, hear you, not judge you, and will understand. I think that's really important.

The other thing is how much of the healing process seems connected to a willingness to be vulnerable with others, and a willingness to reconnect with one's feelings. That has to happen in a place where you feel safe. I know so many times for myself, what I've done for awhile in my life is I would start feeling a feeling and I would find ways to stop it. I would cut it off. It could be anything. It could be a negative feeling, but more often a positive feeling. I would start feeling good about something and I would just cut it off. I don't allow it to come up. And what's been very powerful for me is being willing to allow those feelings to come up and actually express themselves and to share it with someone else, no matter what it is. That's very powerful. It happens in the context of connection and it happens only at a pace you're comfortable with. That feels like the key. That feels like the most important thing.

Chris and I continued to talk. After a few minutes, he wanted to keep recording.

Chris: A really powerful concept is the notion of power and love, and how they relate to one another. There was someone at a male retreat who taught aikido. He talked about a couple of different things. He was teaching people that aikido was a way of reclaiming power, but he was talking a lot about the philosophy behind aikido as well. This seemingly very simple formulation was very powerful to me. His formulation was power plus love equals life.

I guess something very common within survivors is that power takes on a very negative connotation for them. For them...for them? For myself, because I know this is true for myself. Power gets equated with control. It takes on a very negative sense or feeling. I hold myself back a lot, which is something I've struggled with throughout my life.

So in situations, I don't want to take up too much space. I don't want to let my own light shine because I worry that other people will feel bad about it or maybe will attack me because of it. I can think of so many examples in my life when I have not gone after things because I've been afraid of my own power.

This is a newer concept for me. When I think of it and how it relates in my own life, I see it when I talk with other survivors as well. There is this worry about tapping into their power. I notice it with myself. Even when I'm around other people I will defer to people. I'll let them speak instead.

I think it is important to recognize one's power, one's capacities, and one's dreams. We were actually talking about this in the last men's group we had. We were talking about these dreams they had as kids and how they just disappeared. They just seemed like they couldn't even be followed anymore. So for me that's a loss of power. That's a loss of their power; their own belief that they control their world. But they need to understand that their actions matter.

I'm kind of going off on tangents now. This is a bit of a tangent, but that's fine. I am now struggling with a critical part of myself. I know for a lot of my life I dealt with depression, and one of the most frustrating experiences was that it almost seemed like the actions I took in the world didn't matter, because whether I did this or I did that, I would feel like shit. So why put effort into something when I know that I'm just going to feel terrible? I thought, "I'm not going to leave the house. All the work I would have done over three or four days is just going to disappear anyways." And that's such a powerless feeling, a feeling like you didn't have control over your life or your experience.

So the ability to step into one's own power, and recognize that power is not simply...I mean... the way most survivors experience power early on was someone exerting this terrible, unhealthy, abusive sort of power on them. But there's another form of power too.

Whatever gifts we have to bring into the world, our own voice, our own selves, and being willing to step past whatever fear one has, or whatever sort of restricts oneself and stepping into that. That's really important. I mean God, I still battle with that every day in so many different ways. But I know that part is very intimately connected to me; living a life I feel good about.

Me: I believe every person has many different skills and talents, but I argue that a lot of people don't tap into them. I would argue abuse teaches us to not tap into them, which is so unfortunate because you have all of these incredible people throughout the world with all these incredible talents, whether it be art, music, poetry, the gift of speaking, the gift of listening, the gift of healing, whatever it may be, and they don't even come close to tapping into them. So how can you become empowered if you don't tap into what you possess or could possess? Do you believe in empowerment?

Chris: I absolutely do.

Me: How does one become empowered? How do you become empowered? What does empowerment mean to you?

Chris: I think for myself and I think for a lot of survivors, there's so much shame that gets carried around that you become empowered as that shame drops away. I think about leaving that first weekend I went to that first male survivor weekend, and I could feel layers of shame dropping off and dropping away. I would notice that I carried myself differently, that I was almost exhibiting more power, that I sort of held my head up more. I would meet people at the eye more often. So being in a group where I felt more validated, and where I recognized or was better able to recognize, and really feel the fact that this is an experience that I shouldn't have to feel shame about. The abuse was something that was done to me. It doesn't speak to my character. Releasing that shame allowed me to feel like I belonged in the world more. That felt empowering. Being around other people. Being around supportive people. Being around people who are willing to share. I began to see the universality of the effects that this abuse has.

And then you realize that this clearly is not about me. This cannot be about my character. There are thirty men in this room of all different sorts coming from all different walks of life who had this singular experience, and because of this have this very clear set of results and symptoms in their life. You begin to see that this cannot be just me. The power of that is really helpful in removing some of the shame and stepping into one's power.

Chapter 18

FALSE UNITY

———

"Sexual violence is a human problem, and we are not solving anything or even helping society as a whole if we only think sexual violence affects one gender."

As previously stated, Corey and I met before we both spoke at a rally that had a purpose of "ending rape culture". The idea of speaking in front of two hundred people excited me, but also made me nervous. This rally felt truly special to me because I had never participated in a march before and I had never spoken to that many people as an O & E volunteer. I prayed and prepared for days before my speech.

My boss gave me an outline with certain talking points that I complied with, but I wanted to add to the speech. I thought this would be an incredible opportunity to strengthen the people. I wanted to connect to all of them and inspire as many as possible to actively join THP. This rally seemed like the perfect place to ask people to volunteer because these folks were activists who seemed to care about the issue of sexual violence.

After Corey courageously shared his story, a palpable energy infused the crowd. The march began with passion, intensity, and anger. People screamed at the top of their lungs and waved their signs in the air. It was surreal, and I became even more determined.

The experience of marching up the street while listening to people scream about an issue they care about was very new for me and unlike anything I'd experienced during an O & E engagement. The goals I had for the ten minutes I spoke were simple: Inform people of THP's existence and inspire as many participants as possible to get active after the march ended. I wanted to achieve these goals because some people still rape, some people still get raped, and some people will suffer. Some people sadly take pleasure in other people's sufferings. I wanted to fight the evil by empowering the people. I thought to myself, *What better place to utilize their passions than THP?*

We arrived at the second stop of the march for the next speech. I was ready. A woman gave me a megaphone and I began to speak. I first asked the crowd to thank Corey for his strength and courage to share his story. I told everyone it could not have been easy for Corey to do what he did, and that he should be applauded for sharing his story. For some reason the applause was not what I expected it to be. I thought they would have roared like they had earlier, but they did not. I then asked the crowd to give themselves a round of applause for themselves. I told them that they did not have to be there, but they were giving their time to support a great cause, and they too should be applauded. For some reason the applause waned in intensity even more than the first round. The mood in the crowd felt different. The mood changed for reasons I did not know at the time.

I began my speech. I explained the services that THP offers free of charge. I elaborated on the hotline and told them that the hotline receives thousands of calls each year. Only dozens of people take those phone calls. I told them that THP needs some help and I invited them to try and join. I said that every single person's voice matters. Every single person can do this work if he or she wants to. Every single person can play a role in the healing process of a survivor. Every single person can change a person's life. How? Easily. By believing and listening. Anyone can change a person's life if they do these things. It isn't difficult. It is possibly one of the easiest things to do. A person's life will change for the better if people genuinely believe and listen.

I changed gears a bit and began to talk about perpetration. I specifically said that most perpetrators are men, but most men are not perpetrators. After a brief explanation on perpetration, I then started talking about victim blaming and how victim blaming was a driving force for me to get involved with THP. I tried to stress the fact that we have to challenge victim blaming. After about ten minutes, I closed by saying:

> *I want to leave you with a quote. The quote is, "You are the salt of the earth" (Matthew 5:13, New American Bible). Let me say that again. You are the salt of the earth. Think about that…what does that mean? Let me give you my interpretation of what that means. What does salt do? It makes food taste better. For example, I love to cook. I cook mostly Italian food. If I make a sauce with no salt, the sauce is bland. I taste it and say it needs salt. So I add some more salt and it tastes a little better. I taste again. I decide to add more salt so that it will taste even better than before. The sauce is okay, but it can be better. What makes it better? More salt. So I add more salt until the sauce is how I like it. I then cook my pasta and serve to my guests. The food tastes delicious and everyone is happy. The people are happy because they are eating good food. I am happy because I produced a good meal and my guests are happy, relaxed, and satisfied. All it took to produce such happiness, relaxation, and satisfaction is a little salt. The same is true with human beings. We all have the ability and the power to make ourselves, other people, and the world better. I challenge all of you to be the salt of the earth, because you can be. Thank you for listening.*

I handed the megaphone to a woman leading the rally and stood in with the rest of the crowd. Some people clapped. The applause sounded weaker than the previous two times. The mood had shifted noticeably. In my own foolish and naïve mind, I thought they might have been taken aback by my words and demeanor. Maybe I hit them with some knowledge or wisdom and they didn't know how to react. I thought I actually connected to most people. I was wrong.

I later found out that a lot of people hadn't even listened to me. Corey believed they didn't listen to me because I am a man. It didn't matter that I got up there in front of two hundred people in support of them and their rally to speak about an evil in the world. It didn't matter that I had spent my Saturday trying to teach them about THP, support them, and give anyone anything that they needed in terms of emotional and mental support or encouragement. It didn't matter that I've been a trained rape crisis counselor for years. It didn't matter that I have received an obscene amount of rape disclosures throughout my life and have helped people from killing themselves. It didn't matter that I have cried so many times since becoming a rape crisis counselor. Apparently, my gender is what mattered most to the majority. It seemed like they just didn't respect me because I am a man, even though plenty of men participated in the rally that day.

After I finished speaking, a woman got on a microphone and made possibly the worst speech I had ever heard. This woman talked about the prison industrial complex in a very illogical and closed-minded way. She was angry that a town in Massachusetts built a women's jail. She apparently did not understand that some women actually need to be incarcerated. She talked about how so many women are raped in prison, but failed to mention men and adolescent boys. Female prison rape is a serious problem, and I will speak out against rape in female prisons, but for some reason this woman didn't seem to care that men and adolescent boys are also raped while incarcerated. She didn't seem to care that some non-violent men get locked up in violent prisons with violent inmates. She didn't seem to care that some male inmates are raped for years while incarcerated. She didn't seem to care that some male inmates are bought and sold by other inmates and are the sole property of those inmates.

I get very angry when I listen to such ignorance. Yes, rape affects more women than men, but it ultimately affects human beings, and it sure as hell affects men and boys who are incarcerated. Sexual violence is a human problem, and we are not solving anything or even helping society as a whole if we only think sexual violence affects one gender. I hope that Jim, Don, Chris, and the men you will never hear from help us to understand that this too impacts men and boys.

Three people thanked me for speaking throughout the day. Those people were incredibly sweet, and I felt thankful to meet them even if for just a brief moment. I'm sure there were others decent enough to look past my gender and at least listen to a trained rape crisis counselor who has volunteered his time for years trying to help survivors, even if they disagreed with me. But the majority of the people were not able to do that. What truly blew my mind at the end of the day was that out of two hundred people that wanted to "end rape culture", not one person signed up to join THP. Not one.

I believe in hope. Life is very dark without hope, regardless of whether or not you have been raped or sexually assaulted. But I have come to realize that sometimes I am too hopeful. I really thought I would be able to get some names on a piece of paper of people who wanted to volunteer. But not one out of two hundred people did. Not one.

I thought it was pathetic that not *one* person could put a name on a piece of paper to help someone in need, but they could piss every driver off that day by taking down the streets and screaming while holding signs. The whole thing just pissed me off. My anger then turned into sadness. I walked around the area after that rally completely confused and sad. I felt confused because I didn't really understand what I had just spent three hours participating in. I felt saddened because I'd participated in a weird rally with no real purpose, direction, or action.

Corey came to my apartment two weeks later to share his story for this book. After we finished recording, Corey told me there were two articles written on the internet about the rally. Both articles barely mentioned Corey, who was by far the best speaker from the day. That enraged me. He also told me that neither of the articles mentioned that a rape crisis counselor from THP spoke. They completely overlooked me and THP. Corey told me they didn't even put the THP hotline number, office number, or website in the article.

I will never be able to understand how Corey did not receive more recognition for what he said and the guts he had that afternoon. I can slightly understand if those people didn't want to use my name, or even mention me at all, but how could they not even mention THP or list the hotline number? It appalls me that the author or authors didn't have the decency to mention anything about THP. I thought it was pathetic.

Most, if not all of the people in attendance must have benefited from something in that rally. Some may have learned a few new facts. People may have felt empowered. But that rally did nothing to help anyone after it ended. Not one person out of two hundred signed up to volunteer. That rally did nothing to help make connections with THP or outreach to the thousands of people in and around the surrounding area who need help. The least the organizers could have done was list THP's contact information. It would have been so simple, yet they chose not to.

The people's restless, even rude inactivity proved to contradict their stated purpose for assembling. Their own prejudices blind them. This makes them ineffective as fighters in the war against sexual violence. They sadly can't even see the people actually fighting and making a difference right next to them. They alienate a partner in their noisy, self-centered, melodramatic protesting, and accomplish nothing for those they presumably love. That is deeply disheartening to me.

This complete lack of togetherness and unity perpetuates part of the problem. If we can't even share valuable contact information, how are we supposed to outreach, help, and unite with each other? The thought of, *We are all in this together,* is nonsense. I used to believe that people who cared about an issue and got active would band together for the greater good of those they were fighting for, but I have learned over the years that it isn't true all of the time. We will never accomplish anything if we don't work together. If we can't even do the smallest, simplest things like list a phone number or listen to a person that is different than us, how are we supposed to tackle the big problems that affect us all?

Chapter 19

SHIRA

———

"A lot of us have this grand idea of what we're going to do when something like this happens. We think we're going to scream or fight. Very few of us think we'll just freeze – but that's what many survivors do, and that's what I did. I couldn't figure out what was happening."

My experience at that pathetic rally was rare. Most of my time as an O & E volunteer has been very fulfilling and I've been lucky enough to meet some incredible people. In all of my travels and experiences, I have learned an extremely valuable lesson: Things start to change when people start to speak. In my experiences of multiple group settings, I have witnessed one person or multiple people disclose to the whole group after someone else discloses. It's like a chain reaction that occurs. I can't fully explain why it happens, but it happens.

One example of this is when I spoke at a high school. I walked into the room and was greeted with an intense excitement. The students seemed so happy that people from THP had come to speak with the group. Their enthusiasm that day felt much more tangible than at other engagements. I remember thinking that it wasn't that big of a deal for me to speak to the students, but it meant so much to them. Everyone waited in anticipation and eagerness, which ultimately made for a special group discussion.

The discussion unfolded like other engagements, but one woman in the audience became very emotional towards the end. I remember her shaking and crying quietly. Her friend put her arm around her to be consoling. I don't know if anyone else had noticed what was happening, but the discussion continued. This woman finally snapped and said, "I have to say this!" while tears rolled down her face. We stopped the discussion and let her speak. She disclosed that she had been sexually assaulted. She expressed anger at herself for not saying anything while it happened. Based on what I heard, it sounded like she blamed herself.

Everyone in the room listened and gave her a comfortable space to disclose. Some of her peers became counselors and made statements that helped her understand that she was not at fault and there was nothing more she could have done. They did not blame her for what she didn't do. On the contrary, they helped her to realize she is not to blame for anything. After, another woman spoke up and said, "I didn't say anything either, but I say something now."

Similar reactions happened when I first accompanied Shira at a college. This engagement turned out to be my most memorable survivor speaker engagement. The reason it is the most memorable is because of the immediate impact it had on those who participated and listened. Lives appeared to have changed.

While driving to the college, I asked Shira if she was okay. I said, "Are you nervous? What do you need from me? How can I help you? Just give me a look and I'll step in if you don't feel comfortable answering a question." She appreciated my help, but was prepared to tell her story and answer any questions that might be asked.

I helped set up chairs in a giant circle and asked everyone to sit down once the professor told me to do so. The kind professor started our group off by talking about the importance of the day and the college's goals for the session. She then introduced Shira and me. When the time came to begin, I explained THP's services to the participants and then introduced Shira.

Shira began to speak and tell her story. She somehow stayed very calm while talking about a truly horrific rape that she had survived. It amazed me that she spoke so eloquently about what happened to her while others sat and listened. As the accompanier, I had to make sure Shira was okay, but I also observed the room and helped people if they needed to be helped. This night was extremely emotional. Some people started to cry while Shira was speaking. This is Shira's story:

My Story

My name is Shira, and I'm here from THP to tell you my story. Every survivor's experience is different, and mine in particular is very unusual – please keep in mind that I'm speaking solely about myself and my experience.

I was twenty years old and living in Las Vegas, and one night, at about 1am, I decided to go for a walk. The thing about Vegas is that it's a 24-hour town; 1am in Vegas is like 9pm in Massachusetts! And I lived in a pretty safe neighborhood near UNLV. So I went out walking. On my way back home, I took a shortcut behind my usual coffeehouse and someone said hi. It took me a minute to remember who they were, and I said hi back. Close to home, I was still feeling a bit restless, so I decided to go and see if a nearby friend was still awake.

I walked down the sidewalk just two blocks from my apartment, past the empty lot. A guy was parked on the side of the road, leaning against his car – a white 1970s muscle car with gray primer splotches. He nodded and said hi; I said hi back. I didn't recognize him, but it had taken me a minute to recognize the person I saw by the coffeehouse, and I'm generally a friendly person. I kept walking – and as I passed him, he grabbed me from behind with both arms and pulled me into the car.

A lot of us have this grand idea of what we're going to do when something like this happens. We think we're going to scream or fight. Very few of us think we'll just freeze – but that's what many survivors do, and that's what I did. I couldn't figure out what was happening. I couldn't reconcile this with my life experience.

My shoe had fallen off my foot. I remember that. He had gotten in the car and was restraining me with one arm, and I said, "My shoe."

"You don't need your shoe."

"But… if you let me go. Later. If you let me go. I'll need my shoe." He leaned over me. He got my shoe.

He drove me just a few blocks to an apartment building that I was familiar with, one I'd looked at when I first moved to Vegas. He told me to be silent and he pulled me to his door: 117A. My mind was taking snapshots of that door with its peeling red paint, the muscle car, my abductor, his clothing. Just in case he let me go. To this day, over a decade later, I can tell you exactly what he was wearing.

It was a studio apartment. Cluttered. He pulled my clothes off. There was dialogue too banal to recount, phrases he must've pulled from movies – "no one knows you're here", and "I can do anything I want to you", and "if you fight me it'll be worse". I said no. I said no a lot, in so many different ways: "Why are you doing this?" and "Please don't," the whole litany, and it did not matter to him; he pulled off my jeans and my shirt and my panties and my bra.

He tied my wrists behind my back with a dirty white tube sock. He wanted to blindfold me – I convinced him that I couldn't see anything without my glasses, which was true. He used the other sock to gag me.

And then he raped me.

He actually went down on me to try to get me wet, to make it easier for him. Some survivors do respond sexually during rape, because the body can respond independent of the mind. I didn't, though, and *he gave up. The first time he tried to enter me, he almost entered my ass, and I shifted; he slammed me down on the bed and said, "You don't have a choice."*

I didn't fight. Later, the nurse who collected evidence from me praised me for that, for going limp; many rapists are in it for the fight, and me fighting might've gotten him off more. I wasn't thinking about that. I was on autopilot. I just went dead limp, and if that made me more difficult and less satisfying to rape... good, I guess.

The one thing he said that brought me back to myself from my limp and distant state: "You're so good, I'm going to keep you here for a few days."

That sent me right back into my body and into panic because my father was coming to visit in two days. My father was maybe going to be looking for me, and I was going to be tied up in this apartment or dead. And that's when I started crying.

He finished. He took the gag off me.

He reached into the nightstand and pulled out a gun.

He said, "I'm sorry. I know I'm going to hell for this."

I said, "Why do you think that?"

"What?"

"What is hell, to you?"

Something in me was fighting to live, and that something apparently defaults to starting theological discussions.

I didn't realize it at the time, but what I was doing was a pretty good tactic. I got him talking. I kept him talking. For three straight hours. I got him talking about his family, and I talked about mine – but a totally fictionalized version of mine. I claimed to be from New York and have a brother. I didn't want him to have anything of my self that he hadn't already taken. I told him my name was Elizabeth.

And at the end, he was apologizing. He'd never done this before, he said. He'd just had a breakup, and he couldn't sleep, and when he saw me, he snapped and acted on impulse. At the end, he wanted to drive me home, so no one else could grab me. I declined.

"You just don't want me to know where you live," he said.

"That's true."

And he let me go.

I walked to the 7-11 on the corner and asked to borrow a pen and a napkin, and I wrote down everything about him and his apartment that I could remember. I gave the pen back. I walked home. One of my roommates was awake and cooking breakfast. He chattered away at me as usual, but when I didn't respond, he asked, "What's wrong?"

"I was raped," I told him.

Neither of us had a car, so we walked to the hospital, where I scrawled, "I was raped" in tiny letters on the ER's intake form. That hospital didn't handle rape cases, so they paid for a taxi to take us to the hospital that did, and I sat in a narrow corridor fighting the urge to pee and waiting for a nurse.

The cops arrived before the nurse. I gave my statement, all the while eyeing the Coke machine in the hallway and wishing I could have one, but knowing that I had evidence in my mouth and knowing it would only make me need to pee more. The cops were high-pressure.

"Are you going to press charges? Are you pressing charges?"

"I need to talk to my family first!"

At the time, I thought that pressing charges might cost money; I was broke. And of course, if it had cost money, my parents would've paid – but I was in shock. All I knew was that my dad was coming to town and I had to tell my dad. I couldn't think of anything beyond, "I need my dad."

Finally the nurse came. She took me to a private room and collected evidence – my whole body was evidence. She swabbed my chafed mouth and wrists, combed my hair looking for evidence of him – she found it all over me. She kept saying, "We've got him! We've got him!"

every time she found a hair that obviously wasn't mine or a good sample. But all I could think was I don't want him.

And I went home.

My friends supported me. One friend organized a crew of bodyguards to accompany me so I wouldn't need to go anywhere alone. I pushed it all away, as much as I could. I didn't return calls from the cops or the rape crisis center. I needed this not to have happened.

I only stayed in Vegas another month; in the end, I just couldn't be there anymore.

I pushed it all away for years. I was silent for a very long time. After a few years, I began haltingly talking about it. In 2002, I wrote the story of my rape and posted it on my blog – and comments exploded. There were so many people who had never spoken about the rapes and sexual assaults they had experienced – they didn't know they could. They didn't know they weren't alone. They didn't know anyone would listen or believe them.

They didn't know they had a community.

We made a community. And over the years, it's gotten more and more societally acceptable to talk about sexual violence, so that now I'm able to be here with you today.

I've told you about that night. But you should also know this: Yes, the rape destroyed me for a while. Yes, recovery was incredibly lengthy and difficult. But recovery happens. I have a wonderful daughter, a fantastic husband, and a really great life. I am happy and whole. The damage can be healed. It will never not have happened. But you learn to live.

Let's open this up to the Q&A. You can ask me absolutely anything.

Shira answered all of the questions openly and honestly. During the Q and A, one woman got up to leave while she had tears rolling down her cheeks. I got up and tried to console her away from the circle while Shira spoke. She told me her husband had raped her. She had never told anyone before this day. I gave her a tissue and explained that the rape was not her fault and she could heal. She listened, but seemed to ponder my statements unconvinced.

I don't know if she believed me or not, but she listened, and I hope my words struck a chord with her. I asked her if she wanted to talk. She did, but she had to leave because she had something else to do. She told me she wanted to be like Shira. I responded, "You can and you will be."

I asked her if she wanted to take a THP card with the hotline number. She thought about it. I said, "You don't have to call or get counseling. You don't have to do anything. But I want you to take this in case you need it. From now on, you can call a 24-hour hotline or get free counseling. This can happen tonight or in twenty years. But at least you will have the number. The choice is completely yours and you can do whatever you want. Would you like to take the card?" She did take the card as she continued to cry. I thanked her for opening up and told her she is strong. She didn't agree, but I reiterated to her how strong she really was for disclosing. I said, "You will be fine. Trust me, you will be okay. Call THP if you ever need anything."

Chances are good I will never see this woman again. I didn't even know her name, but I know Shira played a role in her healing process. Before that day, she had never told anyone her husband raped her. She didn't even know THP existed. But on that day, among total strangers, she learned there is a 24-hour hotline, free counseling, and other services if she needs them. She learned that a rape crisis center providing free and confidential services exists. She learned that healing is a possibility, evidenced by Shira, when she may not have known that before.

I believe this shows us the power of people's words and hearts. It's amazing that someone's life has the ability to change by meeting a stranger who shares their story. It's also astonishing and comforting that someone's life can change dramatically at no financial cost to them at all. I do not know where this woman's life will lead, but I know something happened that day.

Shira continued to answer questions while I attended to this woman. I sat back down and continued to observe the people once she left the room. Some people were crying, so I got up and gave them napkins from the table. One woman spoke and told everyone that she was also raped by her husband. Shira allowed her to speak and share her story with the group. This woman had also never told anyone that she was raped before this day, and here she was, telling a group of thirty strangers. No one judged her. No one blamed her. No one told her to shut up. No one told her to get over it. We just listened and allowed her to be in a comfortable space to speak and get her thoughts and emotions out.

The woman next to her held her hand and disclosed that she had also been raped. The chain reaction that occurred is hard to explain, but it is powerful to witness. It's especially intense to watch people open up and say things they have never said to anyone before around total strangers. I cannot stress this enough: There really is power in our words. This isn't me believing in nonsense or hoping that we do actually impact people. It is real, and we can impact people if we choose to, as those women who disclosed impacted others on that day.

More questions were asked, and then we wrapped up. The professor running the event thanked us for being there and reminded people about the THP information available for them to take. But the event did not end there. There were some women who wanted to speak with Shira. Shira asked me if I could stay, and I immediately said, "Of course." Shira, me, and four other women sat and talked for the next hour. All four of them disclosed that they had been raped. One woman said to me, "I hope one day I can get to the point Shira is at." I told her she could and that she would. There's not one good reason why she couldn't. If Shira could do it, then she could do it, and every other survivor can do it.

Shira helped those women that day, and hopefully helped those that did not disclose or speak to us for an hour. Just because people did not disclose to Shira or me does not mean there may not have been more survivors in the circle that day. And just because we did not hear verbal affirmation from some people does not mean we did not help in some way, even if in a miniscule way. Always remember that. We cannot necessarily gauge how effective we are if people don't say things like, "Thank you so much. That really helped me." Some people will walk out of a room completely silent and expressionless, but their life may have been changed for the better.

Shira and I left to walk back to my car. I asked Shira if she was okay and she said yes. I gave her a ride back to her home and we talked about the event, THP, music, and random things about ourselves. I remained in awe of Shira and the night we had just had. I said, "Shira, do you understand we just received all of those disclosures and talked for an hour! You meant so much to those people. You were simply amazing. You are a leader for those people, and so many others." She thanked me and said, "That's why I do this." I felt so impressed and inspired by Shira and all of the survivor speakers like her. Shira said to me, "I'm dedicating my life to ending sexual violence."

For the purposes of this book, Shira wanted to share more with you. She does not share what you are about to read during THP survivor speaking engagements, but she believed it was important for you to read here.

The Rest of My Story

My story as I tell it is not the whole story.

When THP teaches us how to tell our stories, they teach us to hit everything into a five-minute speech so we can do a twenty-five minute Q&A. And they teach us to embed "hooks" into our speeches – things that make people curious, to prompt questions. One of the most prominent hooks in my story, for example, is the mention of my father's impending visit. The listener knows that I must have told him. How did he react? Did he support me? These are good first questions, and then we can move on to other questions, some of which are far more personal to the questioner.

But that's not all of my story, either.

I chose this story to tell because it's discrete. It has a clear begin-
ning, middle, and end. It is clearly and unambiguously rape – a small
blonde white girl grabbed off the street by a stranger. That's the narra-
tive that people agree equals rape.

But that isn't all. And I'm working on revising my speech, or con-
structing another one altogether.

Because here's my story.

I was molested as a child by a friend of the family. I later became
involved with his son, who was very abusive (sexually, physically, and
emotionally). My boundaries were fractured at a very young age; for
a very long time, it was difficult for me to realize when an interaction
had crossed the line into sexual assault, because I distrusted all of my
instincts.

When I was nineteen, I was living in a trailer park in North
Carolina, and I had a reputation. I was trying to reclaim my own-
ership of my body, but to some, that just looked like being easy.
So when a male friend was over at my place and we were fooling
around and he started to lift my skirt, I said, "No, I don't want to
do that." He said, "You might as well give it up, or I'm just going to
take it."

And I caved, afraid, remembering that abusive boyfriend. I sent
myself far away and endured it, because I didn't want him to hurt me.

It took me over a decade to realize that that was rape.

Four years later, three years after the rape I give my speech about,
my then-boyfriend and I were hanging out with new friends. I'd kissed
a few of them. Months later, one was visiting Florida and came to our
house; I dozed off on the couch at some point, and my boyfriend left to
do an errand.

I woke up with our "friend's" fingers inside me.

And I pretended to be asleep. I didn't know what to do. I pre-
tended, and then I stretched and he withdrew his fingers and I pre-
tended to wake up, and I pretended that I had no idea what had just

happened. I never told my boyfriend because I'd kissed this guy once in a club and I knew what my boyfriend would say.

It took me over a decade to realize that that was rape.

That boyfriend became my husband the next year. When he raped me, I knew it was rape right away. Even though I wasn't physically fighting him, I knew.

I divorced him. I'm remarried now. My current husband is a great guy, and has been with me through a lot of these concussive realizations, a lot of, "That was totally rape."

I'm not going to continue this list. The point is that I could. The point is that my life, like the lives of so many survivors, is full of experiences like this; full of experiences that we weren't even calling rape.

Because it was fingers, not a penis. Because we were too drunk to consent. Because we didn't scream. Because it wasn't a man. Because it doesn't match that neat little checklist. It has taken decades for us to accept that you can be raped by a friend, that you can be raped by an intimate partner, that you can be raped by someone who isn't male, that men can be raped. There are people out there today who have woken up to someone penetrating them and don't call it rape, because if you call it rape, then you are a Rape Victim, and no one wants to be a victim, especially of rape.

A chilling thought: Given that many people do not name these experiences as rape, how far off are our rape statistics? If we don't name this to ourselves, we're not telling the police, and we're not listing it on surveys.

It has become increasingly important for me to talk about the rest of my story. About being a confused child, about being a teenager who expected nothing better. About freezing when violated in my sleep. About not fighting my ex-husband.

Because for at least 35% of us – at least – these are our stories.

The current of sexual violence and rape culture runs much deeper through the texture of our lives than we have yet to discuss. And we

need to discuss it in order to fight it. Our voices are incredibly impor-
tant; our stories are incredibly important.

I'm also a community education volunteer, like Bobby, and I find
the work that I do in that regard extremely valuable – but I think the
most important work I do for THP is telling my story. Not just telling
it, but actively starting a discussion. I always leave as much time as
possible after my speech to stay and talk. I've had times I've stayed at
a venue for an extra hour, because my speech gave a room full of peo-
ple permission to speak about their own experiences and to find their
support and their community.

When I first started telling my story, one did not talk about rape.
One cloaked it in silence. One certainly did not go into detail – and
then answer questions, and then ask you to talk if you want or need
to. The more time passed, the more natural it becomes that we survi-
vor speakers are here telling our stories. And the more time passes, the
more we're talking about rapes and sexual assaults that people were
reluctant to label as such. Only now are we beginning to get the full
picture of what rape culture truly looks like, of how horrifically perva-
sive it is, of how it has silenced even those of us who do speak out.

I will keep going.
I hope you'll come with me.

Chapter 20

JENEE

"I don't think people need to know a priest, pastor, rabbi, imam, guru, or other leader or guide, but I do think everyone can find empowerment in prayer. And that can be anywhere. I really believe everyone has a "God-consciousness" and can receive spiritual balm for the deepest wounds. I think that we understand somewhere on some level that there is a Creator, or something bigger than us."

I worked in the THP office as a case management intern for nine months and traveled into different communities as an O & E volunteer for almost three years, but I only interviewed potential new volunteers once. Anyone wanting to volunteer at THP has to go through a screening process and be interviewed. I'm thankful I signed up for one of these sessions because that is where I met Jenee.

During these sessions, group leaders discuss their particular group and what a volunteer can expect if they are accepted. When my turn came, I spoke as passionately as possible. I explained to the group what O & E members do and shared how much I loved being a part of O & E. At the end of my five-minute spiel I said, "Everyone at THP, in one way or another, changes a person's life. You also have the ability to change a person's life. If you join THP, I guarantee you will change a person's life." Something I said in those five minutes specifically impacted Jenee. She waited until the end to interview with me.

I quickly learned Jenee was an absolute delight to be around and talk to. Jenee described her genuine concern and care for survivors of sexual violence and her desires to contribute to their help and healing. Our ten minute interview turned into fifteen and easily could have gone for four hours. When I interview, I look for two things: someone who truly cares and someone who has passion. Jenee had both. I immediately knew that I was going to give her the best recommendation possible and hoped that she would be chosen by THP.

Jenee ended up telling me that she originally came to THP that night hoping to rejoin the hotline, but something I said made her change and want to join O & E. She liked the idea of traveling into different communities, educating, and having face-to-face experiences with people. Our conversation then turned into religion and God. Jenee confided in me that she is a Christian woman who believes in Jesus Christ. I said to her that Jesus walked to different communities and interacted with people. In the Bible, he walked and talked. He listened to the people, taught the people, and healed the people. I said that O & E members do the same thing, except they do not have a religious affiliation to the work they do. Jenee agreed and believed joining O & E was what she was called to do at that moment in time.

I was happy for Jenee that she was accepted by THP and ecstatic when I found out her first engagement was with me. We signed up to table a health fair on a Saturday afternoon. Community members came together to partake in a gym that consisted of health education, great music, and dancing. Even Jenee had the itch to leave the table for a brief moment to dance with some of the people.

Everything was peaceful and fun. Everyone seemed to be having a great time, but things immediately became very intense once a woman got triggered at our table. She disclosed to us that she had been raped. She started crying at the table while at least one hundred people were walking around the gym, not having a clue as to this woman's breakdown. I talked with this woman at the table, but noticed her children started to wander off into the crowd.

I started to freak out because I didn't want to leave this woman, but I was worried about her kids. Without me saying a word or even looking at Jenee, I saw Jenee leave the table and attend to the children. Jenee took care of the children and made sure they were safe. As a result of her reacting in the best possible way, I was able to continue speaking with this woman who desperately needed someone to be there in that moment. That is how Jenee is. She is an insightful, observant, and caring woman who understands what is important and will do anything in her power to help anyone she comes across. This woman and I could not thank Jenee enough for doing what she did.

Jenee and I have had great history together, so I asked her if she wanted to share her story for this book. She asked that I meet with her for brunch at a restaurant in a mall. We had a lovely, quiet meal together, but the tables started to fill up. I didn't think she should share such personal information about herself while others were around, so we paid the bill and then sat down in a quiet corner of the mall to record. This is Jenee's story:

Jenee: The first thing that comes into my mind when you describe your book and I think about contributing is what influences my entire life and my story. This greatest of all influences is my relationship with God. Fortunately, I have had an awareness of God and a reliance on Him from the very early days of my life because of my parents. I adopted their faith as my own as early as eight years old, so I try to see everything through the lens of Jesus Christ. This includes His deep love for human beings and the way He forgives our unspeakable wrongs. He is here to heal us. So the frame with which I think about my experiences is simply that. He is what makes this okay.

There is a verse in the Bible from Psalms that says the Lord is close to the broken-hearted and saves those who are crushed in spirit (Psalm 34:19, New American Bible). I embrace that. I've internalized that as a helping truth for getting through the difficult times in my life.

My experiences with sexual assault started when I was thirteen, too young and naive to understand much about what was happening. I had run into the living room from outside at the home of some children I "baby-sat" for and become enchanted by something interesting on TV on my way to the bathroom. I use the word "baby-sat" with air quotes because I was really too young for child care to be a serious responsibility for me. These were family friends from the church my dad pastored and I think the mom thought it would be cute for me to look after their two younger sons from time to time. The much older brother came out of his room at some point and stood with me staring at the screen for a minute. I don't know if I even really noticed him there; I just remember being knocked down on the couch and his hands moving roughly under my shirt, over my shorts, and anywhere off limits they could possibly go. It couldn't have been more than a minute or so in time. He then pulled me back up and muttered, "Sorry about that."

I remember staring at him and finally saying, "Ow!" because he had hurt my arm. He left immediately and I just stood there dumbly rubbing my arm, considering the actors on the screen and trying to process what had happened at the same time. I almost dismissed it as something my brain had made up, something silly. Shock and shame set in when I turned off the TV. I started to whimper mournfully to myself, but I never cried. I have never specifically or in any isolated way cried about that event. I spent the rest of the day complaining to everyone that I'd hurt my arm and might need a brace or X-ray.

I didn't know the words to articulate what had happened and I was afraid of upsetting our parents so I tucked the moment far away. At the time I obviously knew little about the statistic that reports survivors of assault sometimes experience similar assaults at other times in their lives. Somewhere along the way, that was a tough idea to grapple with, particularly because it was a reality for me. Only the unique comfort of God helped me get past the self-blame, confusion, and self-doubt that comes with the unreal repetition of events like these. For me, in all the wondering why, God was near, as promised.

In high school, I sat next to a boy – our seats were toward the back of the room – who took liberties beneath my clothes practically every day. Sometimes the room was full of people, but often dark because we watched documentaries in class a lot. Other times he'd try in the middle of lecture just to see how much he could get away with. I always sat mute, frozen.

At one point, I started cutting class – he found me alone in the building after school and made me return his actions on him as if to punish me. I stopped cutting class after that, but sometimes I was so nervous I deliberately showed up late. He always rewarded me with two distinctively obscene gestures in the halls on days that I came late or left the room without returning. I felt pretty horrified by the whole thing, blamed myself for being a prude, and decided this is just what it means to be a girl. I certainly did not say anything to my parents, my teacher whom I adored, or my twin sister who was also in the class.

Me: Do you mind if I ask why it was so difficult to tell someone? Did it ever enter your mind to tell someone?

Jenee: It certainly came into my mind to but I didn't. I eventually hated myself for not saying anything to him or anyone else. It was unbelievably embarrassing on many, many levels – I couldn't even think of where to begin. Minimizing it in my mind was my only recourse and would spare everyone from discomfort. Plus, this was not my first time in a situation like this; this one was just more ongoing. Not speaking up had already become a habit. Unbelievably, I eventually preferred his silence too. I never wanted to speak to him

*and worried if anyone found out through him, they would all blame
me.*

*Looking back, I definitely feel sympathy for the sad, very young
girl that I was. I remember coping by rationalizing his terrible behavior away through ridiculous lines of thought in my head like, "This
is just his way of trying to ask you out", "This is how love begins for
a lot of girls", or "If you keep wearing super tight jeans, he'll just find
you more disgusting, so maybe don't." The whole thing was constantly
on my mind deep down under the surface, but I ultimately compart-
mentalized it, and focused on sports and academics to hold on to some
semblance of joy.*

Me: Did he want you to keep it a secret? Did he instill a sense of fear?
Did he say something like, "This is between us and no one should know"?

*Jenee: His arrogance instilled a sense of fear. We never spoke of it,
though in groups we acted like acquaintances. It continued all year.
I'm sure my silence completely empowered him. I stiffened, turned into
stone, and let it happen almost every day; no one ever noticed or said
anything to me or him.*

*I don't know how the adults in my school did not see what was
happening. I was such a nerd. I was in the National Honor Society. I
got straight A's. I did my work. I was on student council and I volunteered. And then I started to skip and come late to class, which was so
unlike me. But no one seemed to notice. No one cared enough to ask,
"Is everything okay?"*

*Did people really not see what he was doing to me in class and in
the hallways? Did people really not see such an extreme behavioral
change in me? I used to disassociate a lot, but some things you can't
"act" away. It's one thing for teenagers not to be super communica-
tive, but how could the adults not notice this? The adults did not see
the look in my eyes. They did not see the sadness and panic in my face.
They did not notice the change in my demeanor. For whatever reason,
they just didn't see me. Or maybe they did, but no one ever said any-*

thing to me. Over time, I came to the same conclusion: It doesn't matter if I speak up or stay silent. It's all the same. No one will help me, and ultimately, this is all my fault.

His cruelty with the physical and verbal things outside of class grew, and that was maybe the worst part – the whole sort of hidden-in-plain-viewness of it. I wrote him a letter midway both condemning his actions and begging him to stop because I just couldn't say the words. His only reaction was a laugh the next time he saw me. Nothing changed for an eternity of days; at least that's what it felt like in my mind. Most days I struggled against a deep, deep despair because I felt like people knew what was going on, but no one moved to do anything. It wasn't in my nature to blame others, but it hurt to feel so alone, so even if this was all my delusion that they knew, I nurtured that and still sometimes think of it now.

We were talking about the THP survivor speakers earlier. I'll never forget going through the training. On the Wednesday of the training, I listened to Corey share his story. He described that he sat very still and very frozen during his assault. He just froze. He couldn't do anything. He was screaming on the inside but he couldn't seem to do anything. That so resonated with me. It's identical to what happened to me right from the start at thirteen, and then at sixteen. I think the shock and confusion paralyzed me. Hearing his similar story at the training totally and profoundly opened up something for me. I realized I wasn't the only one who had unconsciously become paralyzed when all the time my brain raged to fight back and reclaim my dignity. I can't really express to you what that meant to me. Corey, so many years later from my time in high school, said the thing that finally made me feel less ashamed. Isn't that amazing?

Me: Yes it is.

Jenee: Interestingly enough, the thing that stopped him just before the end of the year is I got a boyfriend. This actually is funny – the boyfriend was a very popular athlete who really just wanted another athlete to go to prom with him, so we convinced ourselves we were in love a month before the big dance. The existence of the boyfriend must have scared the person hurting me because after seeing us together he stopped abruptly. I'm not sure I understood or understand that reaction now, but it temporarily lifted an indescribable weight. From then on the logic seemed like a simple incontrovertible truth in my mind: A boyfriend equals protection, so I should and must always have one.

A year or so into college I learned that the kid who wrecked my junior year had been arrested for assaulting women on a college campus. I had never imagined that the ramifications of my silence might be that the same thing could happen to someone else with this person. This was, and still is, an awful feeling. There is some shame and guilt about that. I don't know that my words would have stopped those assaults, but I sometimes wonder.

Me: It wasn't your responsibility to stop those assaults from happening. He chose to assault. You shouldn't feel shame and guilt about that.

Jenee: You're right. I know you're right. Thanks for saying that. All of this reminds me we have to do more about helping people affected by sexual assault get beyond the original undeserved shame and then the shame of staying silent. It can take a long time – it has for me – but I've come to realize the power in owning the painful experiences out loud. It's really a scary thing to do. Any support we can give children in particular to not be ashamed and know they will be believed and loved desperately if they have something to share, we must. We must give each other that support.

I remember having this locked-up, everything shut-up feeling around this seemingly unspeakable thing. I was like a condemned house, all boarded up and awful. I stayed mute for so long, well into adulthood, about the terrible behavior from him for a million reasons. At the time those reasons ranged from not having the awareness, language, or courage to identify it as sexual assault to horror at my unrecognizable ongoing chicken reaction.

I also kept quiet because of unchangeable parts of my personality that balked at the idea of making people sad around me and really being a nice girl at my core. I didn't speak because I no longer wanted to live inside my own skin – I felt so gross, and I couldn't talk about me. Just one word out loud and something might break forever.

Despite my knowledge of the love God has for us, I felt something had spun out of control when I wasn't paying attention – this was a shortcoming in myself the oblivious adult world just should not know. So, rather than talking, I decided to not be very nice to me. I'd say to myself, "You should have known better than to have gotten yourself into a situation like this. A good Christian girl…shame on you, allowing these things."

I think it's possible that others might be able to relate to some of these responses. So we must do a better job of sharing this message in the lives of everyone we know and the whole world that a survivor of sexual assault is never to blame. We must believe and support when he or she speaks out. It breaks my heart to think of people suffering silently or alone with this. It is unfair that the survivor has to live with the fear of external and internal judgment, ceaseless worries about how the next sexual situation will go, and whether he or she will ever really feel completely okay.

I do not believe most people talk about this. It's not just the survivor who stays quiet – the whole issue is shrouded in silence, and there is so much negative attention toward the survivor. If you've been assaulted, the unknown of what happens upon speaking up is just as trauma-inducing and imprisoning as the event itself. For a long time, that's the way it felt for me.

The good news though, is despite all that, God has a way of weaving a hope and compassion for ourselves in our hearts if we open them to Him. It's a work in progress that begins as soon as we surrender and allow that. God makes the difference for me. He helps me achieve distance and perspective on situations like the one I just described.

Now that I am older, I can think about how I am growing with God's grace into a better version of myself. The person in my high school must have been pretty lost, even tormented to continue the way he did. I don't think he had an understanding of the ramifications of his choices for either of us. I think that's sad. He may not have felt regret or remorse, but whatever was going on for him, I feel sorry for him if he does not have a relationship with God now.

Obviously these kinds of things stay with you, whether you're the perpetrator or the survivor. But I'm in such a better place than I was – not because there is anything special about me – but because God has extended His grace and love over and over. I love reading passages in the Bible that talk about how He's a healer and how He is close to us. There is nowhere we can go to be out of His reach. Ultimately, if we find ourselves desperate for healing, no matter what that looks like getting there, He has love, mercy, and kindness to help. I've internalized all that. I've received all that. Even ways in which experiences negatively impact relationships in the future, I thank God that I have Him to go through that with. I feel sorry for the individuals that have harmed me through assault and don't have God's peace. I wish that peace for them.

Me: So you feel empathetic towards the people who abused you?

Jenee: Yeah.

Me: You're not angry towards them?

Jenee: No. Not usually. I've decided to not let their actions define mine. I think I wonder why more than I feel anger – I find it all sad and puzzling, but maybe, maybe explainable. All of these people were slightly older than me, but young enough to still have some growing to do. I'm not talking about a situation where the perpetrator is an older relative, which in my mind is far worse than anything I went through. But I wonder if these people were just foolish and immature and mean because their minds and capacities for empathy hadn't developed appropriately yet. I don't know, I might be completely wrong. I believe in rehabilitation and redemption though. I think God is a big part of that.

Me: Rehabilitation and redemption is there for those who want it. Not everyone wants it.

Jenee: I think that is true for sure. But I also believe every human being has a God desire or higher power consciousness, even if he or she is not specifically cognizant of it or chooses not to pursue it. You and I have spoken a lot about the concept of healing. I believe God is critical to that healing. Maybe I am delusional in terms of the people who took awful advantage of me – it's possible, and clear in one case, I am not the only person they hurt. If they find themselves remembering back to those moments, the feelings that come up cannot be very good ones. Honestly, I hope they find a healing relationship with the Lord if they haven't found one already.

Me: You might be right that every human has a God desire or higher power consciousness. Maybe we will never know whether that is true or not. I personally believe we are all God's children and that God is in our hearts. Yet I also know there are many who do not believe in God, and some who commit acts of violence in the name of God. Some people use God to manipulate, condemn, hurt, rape, and commit other atrocities. It makes me very angry and sad.

I believe human beings have free will and that we all make choices. The people who hurt you made choices to hurt you. You say that you are not angry towards your perpetrators. Did you ever get angry towards them?

Jenee: I was always sad more than any substantial anger. I can't stay mad for long for some reason, but I can stay sad for a long time. If I get mad it's more at myself. For me, all of this is very complicated because I assumed the victim role during childhood and never let it go. I drifted into two adult situations expecting to be treated badly in terms of "intimacy", and that is what happened. I unfortunately fully expected sexual assaults to occur in those situations because that was my way of looking at the world of men; I headed straight for them and I was right.

Maybe I thought if I could convince myself I "picked" these people, which wasn't the case really at all, I'd have at least some sort of control with them. That was a joke, and looking back, pretty sick thinking. I should say I understand what I was doing now and also how flawed my vision was. I want to also say that I had some good relationships with men and there are many more good men than not in the world. Every day I am lucky enough to have several of the best good men God ever made in my life. I am truly blessed.

However, in terms of the other, I resigned myself. I gave up fighting because things seemed familiar, and I was still paralyzed from when I was thirteen. I was sad underneath and lost sight of who was to blame. I unfortunately blamed myself and not the people who hurt me. I was angry at myself. I just passively hated myself. Does that make any sense? Can you see how you can get to a place where you really hate yourself and you are so mad at yourself for a hundred compounding reasons that you choose to stay in pathetic situations that will only make you feel worse because you're just that deeply miserable?

Me: Of course it makes sense. I have met many people throughout my life who have been just like you; sexual abuse survivor or not.

Jenee: Rehashing the bad memories that started things off can make you feel as vulnerable as a nervous little teenager again...

(Jenee began to break down)

Me: Are you okay?

Jenee: I'm okay.

Me: You love God. There are billions of people who believe in God. So what does it feel like to have such a loving, healing relationship with God that you speak of? How has that healing been real to you? Is it an internal peace in the mind? In the body? Is it something else?

Jenee: It's pretty transcendent. You use the words "internal peace" which reminds me of a verse in the New Testament book of

Philippians that describes a peace that passes all understanding (Philippians 4:7, New American Bible). By definition, it's almost impossible to explain! Somehow, after regular communicating with God, reading the Bible, and surrounding myself with positive people, I feel it. A lot of people call it meditation. For me, my communication with God is about relationship. I find myself listening for His calming ways when I pour out my thoughts to Him. Inevitably, I feel that healing. I feel that empathy that I don't know for sure is necessarily germane to human nature. I don't think the empathy I feel has anything to do with something good about me – I think God gives us that sort of compassion for others. Hopefully this answers your question: The short summary is Jesus makes all the difference for me. He makes forgiveness and impossible peace possible.

Me: You started at THP on the hotline. You first met me years later and there was something I said in five minutes that made you want to work with people face to face as an O & E volunteer. We have worked together, and I see that you clearly have the passion for this work. Why? What is it that you want to do for people? How do you want to teach and help others?

Jenee: So let me first back up and describe what happened for me when I heard you speak about O & E. I had been thinking about returning to THP for a while, but I waited literally years for the timing to feel right. So I showed up at this orientation session for potential volunteers believing I would interview for a hotline counselor position again. I wanted to get a sense of how things had changed and the new people now a part of this work, as THP had been very important to me when I volunteered in college.

So representatives from every department shared about their focus area and then you spoke. Something happened. I'm smiling remembering the way it felt to hear and watch you share your passion for the work of THP at large and the O & E side of things. I was transfixed, as was everyone in the room. You had an energy and earnestness that you conveyed through compelling language for the importance of educating people about the issue of sexual assault and increasing aware-

ness about prevention strategies as well as THP services. You shared
about the boots-on-the-ground work of meeting people where they are,
face-to-face, and the joy and power that is in all of that.

You mentioned how frequently you volunteered at events and that
this work had been more fulfilling than your day job because this was
about helping people. It was clear to see in your expression that the O
& E experience had been transformative in your life as much as your
work with others had blessed them (although you were more humble
about that part). Beyond your actual words, I could see the compassion in you and the genuine devotion you have for making a difference
every day in terms of sexual violence. You were unscripted, speaking
from the heart, completely moving in your humility and passion for
what you do as an O & E volunteer.

At the end, you shared in humble tones that this had been for you,
and would be for us, an experience to positively change someone's life.
You paused and let those words sink in. I remember hearing something
in your voice when you spoke again that suggested that this – impacting a fellow human being's life from a place of caring and concern by
sharing good news of hope and un-waning support for them – is the
greatest blessing any of us can give or receive. I'll never forget it; I was
totally inspired and very blessed. Looking back at that night, I can
only think of the timing as serendipitous (my students love this word)!
If not for you, I'm pretty confident I would have volunteered for a hotline position. So before I answer the question you just asked, I want to
say thank you for motivating me and other volunteers on our journeys
in trying to help others.

Me: Thank you, Jenee. That means a lot. But I don't want what you just
said in the book.

Jenee: This is how it was for me and this is my story so you have
to leave it alone! One other thing I'll say is that interviewing with
you was unlike any interview I've ever had! It was also markedly
different from my first interview with THP back in the day. Usually,

the interviewee feels nervous and concerned about impressing the interviewer, but you exuded approachability and super-coolness so I was just excited to talk to you about our shared passion for this work. I had no trouble feeling I could be transparent about my faith and family commitments while we "interviewed". I remember talking of rape crisis issues comfortably like old, familiar friends. You grabbed a napkin, and in thoughtfully spontaneous Bobby-style, wrote down the titles of two inspiring books for me to read! It was really awesome!

Talking with you about all of this now helps me to think about the roots of my passion for this work and the whys of some of my choices in college and grad school. My freshman year was at a historically black college in Maryland where I went to find identity and comfort. I instead felt jumpy at cat calls, suspicious of male attention, and unnerved by all the "brothers" who could never manage to look me in the eyes, even during the most casual conversations.

I transferred to college in Massachusetts, not necessarily for these reasons, and joined the campus sexual assault network and hotline. Hotline was a deliberate and ironic choice – I think I was drawn to the private-ness of it, the secrecy of the communication on both ends of the phone. I always took the weekend, midnight to 7am shifts, the saddest and loneliest hours on earth if you're sad and lonely. I never slept (just like I don't sleep now)!

Subconsciously, I wanted to be alert to validate the huge step that people I deemed braver than me had taken in sharing their stories and maybe atone in some way for my silence by hearing them, believing them, weeping with them, laughing with them, raging with them, comforting them with all of my heart's best words. I wanted to whisper in the quiet night that I would always pray for them, that God would surely help somehow, and so I did; though this was not part of the suggested script from my gigantic, red THP binder. Maybe this explains a little about where my passion comes from.

I don't know what drives people to want to absorb the pain of complete strangers on a crisis phone call, but I know why I needed to, and I know what it felt like to be in that moment with a beautiful soul I believed I understood a little. My motivation was simply love, connection, and compassion every single time. Sometimes I dared to illegally say, "I am here for you right now. Whatever you need. I have great knock-knock jokes. Or we can just be quiet. But when I go, I'm going to leave you in God's hands because I just know, I really know that He will take better care of you." It was like my mantra to soothe both of us, all of us, even during the calls when I didn't say that out loud. So I listened out for them – my phone friends, my peeps down in the struggle, my sisters and brothers, my kin – for three intense years.

I ended my time on hotline and at THP with many, many calls from one seventeen year-old girl who had been raped and abandoned and chose me to cling to. Her crushing story broke me a little. Her personality reminded me of seventeen year-old me. I turned her case over to the director of THP, changed my cell phone number which I had broken the rules in giving her, and walked away somewhat damaged myself. But happily, a number of years later, I returned and got to meet you and the O & E team! So, to answer your question, I still want to help people find a way to peace and healing and I still want to whisper my prayers to God for them, not internally but face to face. I want to tell them, as I recall their faces in my mind, that He will surely help somehow. For me personally, God is the best path to wholeness that I have ever found.

Me: I believe God exists. I already mentioned that billions of people believe God exists. I believe it hurts God when we are hurt and when we hurt others, and I believe it makes God happy when we love each other and treat others the way we want to be treated. God did not create us to be miserable. I believe God is love and mercy. No one said life was easy, but I don't believe we are supposed to live a life of suffering without any joy.

Jenee: God did not intend for any of us to live our time in this world, on this earth, in constant pain and in suffering. I think God's love is best shown through human beings. Of course nature obviously shows God's love, but I think people helping people is the greatest expression of God's love. I believe each of us is here to help one another and reach out for each other, trying to get through life together as best we can.

Me: You are a Christian woman. You are part of a non-denominational church, right?

Jenee: Yes.

Me: You seem to be more about the "spirit" and the "church as a community" rather than the "institution of the Church". There are some Christians who say they believe in Jesus but do not seem to have much of an understanding of what He preached and did. There are billions of people throughout the world who do not believe in Jesus. There are also people throughout the world who have never even heard of Jesus. I believe God is in everyone's heart, even though that may be hard to believe with some people. Anyone, atheist or believer, no matter what religion one belongs to, can choose to accept God's existence, love, and mercy. Every believer and non-believer is God's child. I believe it is us who choose to reject God, not God who rejects us.

I said this to you the first time we met because you brought up Jesus: Jesus was a man. He suffered like a man. He walked, He talked, He listened to the people, and He healed the people. That is in the Gospels. THP does the same thing; they just don't have a religious affiliation to what they do. O & E members travel, teach, help, and heal.

Jenee: That is what drew me to O & E.

Me: To me, we are just a pen in God's hand. You say that we are supposed to help each other. Things change when we help each other.

Jenee: Absolutely. So this is my truth: I don't think that my experiences are any worse or better than anybody else's. I don't think I've figured this whole thing out and I know I need the insights and support of loved ones, and just people, to make it. But I do think I have something to offer. I think everybody does. If in some way a person feels like he or she has gotten some traction on the pain and has some sense of balance, I think it's important to share that with others. My message to people still in the early stages of battling the fallout from sexual assault is this: You may not be there yet, but you will get there. You can do this. You've got a never-going-away cheering section in your corner and our voices are loud. A few of us have been through some of these things and we've shown up to help you bear your burdens. There is love left for you, and we're here to stand by you.

Me: Is there anything else that you want to say to say? What is one final thing you want people to know?

Jenee: I just want to emphasize that tomorrow really is another day. There is healing available. There is peace and joy available. You can decide in a minute that you will get through this, and even though it will take longer once that decision is made, you can make up your mind that you're going to get through it in a minute's time. You don't have to wait to decide to reclaim control. You can do it in a minute. There is a process after that and there are people around immediately to help if you reach out.

I don't think people need to know a priest, pastor, rabbi, imam, guru, or other leader or guide, but I do think everyone can find empowerment in prayer. And that can be anywhere. As I've said already, I really believe everyone has a "God-consciousness" and can receive spiritual balm for the deepest wounds. I think that we understand somewhere on some level that there is a Creator, or something bigger than us. Something that can help us make sense of our lives better than we can on our own.

Me: A force greater than us.

Jenee: Exactly. I believe even atheists sense that force. I would say, spend some time trying to commune with God, or whatever you want to call that force. I think the one who seeks will find. Also, do all the healthy things that make you happy and calm like running or writing or creating beauty in all the brilliant ways you know how to. Pay forward the blessings you have received. There's nothing like doing something for someone else to get you past your problems and adjust your perspective. Listen to great music, visit nearby natural wonders as close as your own back yard, play air guitar, paint your toenails turquoise, dance, adopt a puppy. Make peace with all people if you can, and especially, make peace with yourself. Always know there are friends somewhere rooting for you. There are people you don't know, always praying for you and lifting you before God.

Chapter 21

FORGIVENESS

———

"I talked with my parents and they convinced me that this was not my fault and had I not acted, she might not have been found alive. My parents said to me that any action I took would not undo the harm done to my sister and would not make her better. They gave me the rational answer that my harming him would send me to prison and they would have two victims of this terrible crime. I listened to them, but I really wanted to choke the shit out of him. My mother explained that my hate would put me in a prison of my own making, not the person who did this to my sister."

I have met many different people throughout my journey as a rape crisis counselor and writing this book. One man who has been a light to me is Timothy. Timothy is one of the smartest people I have ever known. He is a man that radiates peace, compassion, light, and love. Those who interact with him know how gentle yet strong he really is. I have been blessed to know Timothy and thankful that he has educated, challenged, strengthened, inspired, and helped me throughout tough times in my life.

Timothy and I have had a decent amount of communication through-out the writing of this book. I would occasionally ask for his opinions and guidance throughout this process, and he always made time to listen to me. Timothy often inspired me to keep writing. He would say, "This book has to be spread." He always cared about the issue of sexual violence, but in all the years I have known him and all the conversations we have had, I never knew that he too was impacted by this evil crime until he read the introduction to this book. The words I wrote hit him somewhere deep, and he felt compelled to write for himself. He gently asked me one day, "Do you have room for another story?" Not knowing what he even meant, I said, "For you? Anything."

I was taken aback by Timothy's request. He had never talked about his family in all the years I've been speaking to him about my experiences at THP. He never once asked to contribute anything in the two and a half years he has heard about this book. I had no idea the introduction would ignite emotions and memories in Timothy that made him look deep within himself and write something he felt he needed to write. I had no idea the introduction made him realize that he has been holding onto bitter pain and that he felt the need to forgive.

You have met the survivors who wanted to contribute and share their stories in their own words. What has not been discussed in this book is how significant others are also impacted by sexual violence. I cannot com-prehend how many people throughout the world know of someone who has been raped or sexually assaulted, but I know there are too many. This is one story of one man who believed he did not protect someone he loves. This is Timothy's story:

Timothy: I grew up in a household with two parents and one sister. As an older brother, it was expected of me to protect my younger sister from harm. This was an expectation that men throughout my community held. I took my role seriously and my parents and my sister appreciated the fact that I looked after my sister.

My sister was three years younger than me, and had started as a freshman at college as I started my senior year in college. My sister was also protected from "street life", and did not go to clubs or hang out with "women wise in the ways of the world".

Since she lived at home, there were no warnings given about men she knew, only about men she did not know. She was a virgin and intended to marry as a virgin because that is what was taught in our schools and churches at the time. My father was always respectful of my mother and my sister's expectation was that she would marry a man who was respectful of her.

Then one afternoon as she was waiting for one of my parents to pick her up to bring her home, someone she knew from a class offered to give her a ride home. Only he took her to his house. This person was not a friend of mine or even an acquaintance, just someone going to college like I was going to college. But that evening he raped my sister.

When she was not at the place my parents were to pick her up, they started calling others in our neighborhood who might have given her a ride. When that did not indicate where she was, I started calling my friends to see if they had picked her up or knew of someone who had picked her up. One of my friends called me and told me the house where she had been taken. I remember my parents and me going to the house and calling her name. She came out after a few minutes of calling, her clothes torn, hair a mess, and bruises on her face and arms.

My little sister was almost catatonic, refusing to talk to anyone. My parents did not know what to do. She just sat in her room. Sometimes she cried and sometimes she just sat in her room and looked out the window. My parents soon brought her to the doctors to counsel her to get over the experience. The doctors said a criminal case was useless because she could never stand to be questioned by the police or the defense attorney. They finally gave her shock therapy to get her out of the mental rut she was in. She was never completely herself again.

My immediate thoughts and actions were for my sister's recovery and well-being. As time went on I became angry because I could not protect my little sister. I wanted to harm the person who had done this and spent a great deal of my waking hours thinking of ways to hurt but not kill him. I thought castration would allow him to live, but never be able to hurt anyone else in this way.

I talked with my parents and they convinced me that this was not my fault, and had I not acted, she might not have been found alive. My parents said to me that any action I took would not undo the harm done to my sister and would not make her better. They gave me the rational answer that my harming him would send me to prison and they would have two victims of this terrible crime. I listened to them, but I really wanted to choke the shit out of him. My mother explained that my hate would put me in a prison of my own making, not the person who did this to my sister. My mother said that his ultimate punishment would be far worse than anything I could dish out to him.

I resolved to be a committee of one to always act in a respectable way towards women in general, but to always believe that no means no. Coercion of any type is rape. Sex should be fun. It is something that should be desired and enjoyed by both people.

My little sister passed away over ten years ago. I don't believe she ever trusted men again. I do know she never trusted me to protect her. Today, I teach my sons to always respect women; no means no <u>at whatever point it is expressed</u>. I teach them to never ever strike a woman in anger and that sex should be fun, but it is not fun if it hurts either person. Lastly, be able to forgive their attacker for the survivor's sake, not the perpetrator's.

Reading Timothy's story made me contemplate the idea of what forgiveness means. *What does forgiveness mean to me? What does forgiveness mean to the survivors? What does forgiveness mean to every single human being?*

What if we are not able to forgive? Does it hurt or affect us in the short and long term? If so, how does it hurt or affect us? Does it help people who are able to forgive, regardless of what they are forgiving? If so, how is it helpful? Ultimately, what are the impacts on our lives if we forgive or don't forgive?

Justice is different for everyone. Growth is different for everyone. Healing is different for everyone. Sexual violence is different for everyone. People may share similar experiences and even effects, but everyone's story is their own. The same is true for forgiveness. I firmly believe the most effective way to discuss what forgiveness means for the purposes of this book is by having the survivors who already shared their stories explain what it means to them.

This is what forgiveness means to Corey:

Corey: *I see forgiveness primarily as the act of letting go of intense resentment and anger towards the person who abused me, while still acknowledging that the abuse happened. It is about making the choice to put some distance between yourself and what happened. Forgiveness is a choice you can make when you're ready, choosing how much power this person's actions have on your life.*

For me, forgiveness was a step toward healing. It is totally understandable that you might have a hard time letting go of resentment or painful memories of what someone did to you, but at some point it hurts more to hold onto those things. It's not the strictest definition of the word; more like the process of refusing to be very angry or upset about something than to pardon the abuse. I do have control over how being sexually assaulted affects my life.

I have forgiven him in my own way, though I am fairly certain that I will never fully pardon what he did. I think going to court helped the forgiveness process, and him being accountable in some ways helped with some of the pain and anger I was feeling. I think having time lends itself to forgiveness. I couldn't imagine still being in the dark place that I was right after it happened, nor would I want to be now.

This is what forgiveness means to Don:

Don: I had a difficult time getting started writing about forgiveness. What is it and how do I utilize it? In my family of origin, I have much anger/rage about being raised in a violent alcoholic home (and with the very strong possibility they knew about abuse and did nothing). I now know my parents each came from violent alcoholic homes and they did the best they could with what they had. How can I ask them to give me what they never had themselves?

I learned in AA to say a prayer for someone I have resentment towards. Because I can feel the emotions, I can mean and feel the prayers of forgiveness. They are not empty words. I still feel lots of anger towards my family, but those feelings, although still strong sometimes, have decreased exponentially over the years. I can honestly say that the forgiveness process has definitely begun and will continue.

Forgiveness around my abuser is more complex and difficult. I did not fully remember my abuse until I was fifty-eight years old (in 2005); my abuser also died in that same year. I feel totally numb emotionally toward him. I am not even able to be angry at him, so for me to forgive him now would be a pretty cheap forgiveness i.e., an unfelt, intellectual, empty gesture. I have tried to ignite some emotional fire by visiting his grave several times. The first time I tried I did not even get close to it. It was as if there was a barbed wire fence or a force field around the gravesite. I have been there a few times since, but the best I have been able to do is just walk by. The only emotion I feel is fear. I am still partially frozen inside, but as I continue to heal and pray, that fear will continue to melt and I will hopefully be able to make an act of forgiveness and mean it.

It is important for me also to mention that I remember the horrible, animalistic noises he was making while he was penetrating me. They were horrendous, and I realize that the experience may have been as painful for him as it was for me. I can empathize with him a little. What happened to him that caused him to feel that pain and do such horrible acts? Hurt people hurt people. That doesn't excuse the behavior, but it helps explain it. Maybe that bit of empathy I feel toward him is the beginning of forgiveness.

I have learned other helpful tools along the way, one of which is the Serenity Prayer. I cannot change the fact that I was sexually abused beginning at age four. What I do have the power to change is some of the resulting negative, self-destructive behaviors i.e., lack of trust and intimacy, anxiety, low self-esteem, depression, etc. The good news is I have changed by being more trusting and open, calmer and more centered, and most of all, I have remained sober. Recovery from childhood sexual abuse is a long and sometimes difficult road, but all the work I have done (with help) has produced many positive life affirming behaviors. For that I am extremely grateful.

Over the past several years, with lots of help, I have been able to understand in my gut, not just in my brain, that I was not responsible for any of the sexual assaults I endured. I was victimized by a predator and there was nothing at all I could do about it (there's acceptance again). That realization has greatly reduced my shame and guilt and allowed me to forgive myself. I read somewhere that there can be no healing without self-forgiveness, so I guess I am on the right track.

This what forgiveness means to Shira:

Shira: Despite everything, I still believe in forgiveness.

When I was molested as a child, I told my mother. She chose not to believe me, just as my abuser had said. I struggled for years with this – with my feelings of betrayal and, eventually, anger. It took me maybe twenty years to really figure out how she could have ignored the abuse. My mother has a very set-in-stone image of what her life is and, by extension, what her children's lives are. She'll only recognize things that fit into her worldview. I had to come out as bisexual four times before she stopped "forgetting" – a non-heterosexual child didn't fit into her worldview.

The idea that her child could be raped didn't fit into her worldview.

Even more so, the idea that she could be ignorant of it, and then that she could be aware of it and not act immediately to stop it, did not fit into her concept of herself.

So she cut it out of her mind.

In the years since, she has become more aware of this; we don't talk about it openly. We speak in code-phrases. She's still not able to say the words. She still has a difficult time understanding how all of this had happened.

There is no excuse for this, for this failure to protect one's child, for this failure to listen and to stop the abuse. But I realized that carrying that anger was hurting me. It wasn't doing a damn thing to her, but it was actively damaging me.

Part of the forgiveness process, after all, is learning to forgive yourself – overcoming the internalized self-blame many survivors deal with.

So I forgave her. I accepted that I would never have had a better mother, and there was nothing I could do about it now. I accepted her for who she is. I laid down that pile of anger, and I found an unexpected serenity.

This is what forgiveness means to Rebecca:

Becca: Forgiveness…it's a word that means something different to everyone. As a sexual assault survivor, it was one of the hardest things to come by. Because how can you forgive a man who took away your sense of security and another man who took away your faith in relationships and people? I came to realize that in order to forgive doesn't mean you have to forget what they did to you. You'll never forget what happened – but it doesn't have to define who you are.

In my case, it wasn't just the guy who assaulted me that I had to forgive; it was the whole system and student body that didn't believe me. To be completely honest, it was harder to forgive the system because it was supposed to protect me and be neutral. It was hard to forgive the people who talked about me and called me a whore and friends who weren't there for me. It's hard to bounce back when you lose your faith in people, but it's not impossible. In every dark cloud there's a silver lining.

Don't let your anger cause you to forget the people who were there for you when no one else was. I'll never forget the hours Todd spent with me so I wasn't alone. I'll never forget my best friend from home (who was mad at me at the time for something unrelated) putting her anger aside in order to be there for me and go with me to the interview at the police station so I didn't have to face it alone. Those people are the ones you need in your life. Those people will restore your faith in people and make it easier for you to forgive, so surround yourself with those who truly care.

The most important thing to remember if you or someone you know has been a victim of domestic or sexual violence is this – don't confuse forgiveness with weakness. Anger and hatred weigh you down and stress you out. Believe me, I know! I'm not saying that suddenly you'll be stress free and forget the whole thing – I'm saying <u>forgiveness makes you stronger.</u> It's one of the hardest things to do – but it's worth *it. Life never gives you more than you can handle; at times it may seem false, but it will all work out in the end. You'll always have the chance to take something negative and turn it into something positive – starting with forgiveness.*

Always smile, because life gives you so many things to smile about.

Love,

Becca

This is what forgiveness means to Megan.

Megan: To those reading who are survivors (and anyone who knows a survivor): I don't know how to tell you this because I want to be kind, but I want to be honest. If you're anything like me, you'll never forget the person or persons who violated you; who took the person you are and splintered you into pieces before leaving you to clean up the mess on your own. I hope you have people in your life who are helping you pick up those pieces, but I know that sometimes it still feels like you're all alone. That feeling passes, I promise.

On the subject of forgiveness, I have only this to say: You may never forgive him/her/them (allow me to settle on 'them' as I speak with my own situation in mind), you may never forget them, but there will come a time when they – and what they did to you – will no longer define you. You won't feel any more like you have to tell every person you meet or every person you date about that night, that year, that time of your life when you were taken advantage of and hurt. They won't be around every corner – in the world or in your mind. They will no longer be everything you have nightmares about.

If you were sexually assaulted by a close friend, family member, or significant other as I was, you may even come to a place where you can separate the good things from the bad. I can look at the nice things my ex-boyfriend and I did together and say, "Hey, that was nice," without that feeling like a reflection on him (I do not believe him to be nice) or like a betrayal to the truth of what he did to me (our trip to DC does not make the fact that he raped me okay). I can look at the man who taught me to sing AND saved my mother's life before molesting me and be grateful for those good things while simultaneously understanding that that doesn't make him okay. But I'll never forget. You'll never forget. You may be at a time in your healing where that feels like a death sentence.

You may be at that point where you just don't want anything to do with them ever again, and that's okay. Be in that place. Savor that place. Live in that place. And then move forward. Because the one thing I can tell you about that place is that actively hating someone takes a lot of energy and a lot of time that you could be devoting to something, anything, else. They do not deserve your energy or your time. You deserve to be happy. To be whole. To not feel broken all the time. And you'll get there. This may be getting to a cheesy point because I'm getting into that "message of hope" thing, but the message remains the same: It may feel like a long road – a road that doesn't conform to your preferred timeline – but there is an endpoint, a light at the end of the tunnel, a stopping place.

I want to leave you with a piece of advice my mother gave me many years ago: Ducks survive in the ocean because they dive under waves and when they come up they shake their feathers and the water falls away. Learn from ducks. "Make like a duck," Mom says, "because ducks let the waves wash over them and never let their feathers stay ruffled." Thanks, Mom.

Love,
Megan

This is what forgiveness means to Jenee:

Jenee: I believe forgiveness is the deliberate act of shaking off the things that bind and embracing freedom. For me, it is an insistence on peace at all costs, and I believe the person who fully chooses it demonstrates the most amazing strength of heart. I believe forgiveness has very little to do with the person in the wrong; it has everything to do with the individual who has been hurt.

My ultimate reference point for forgiveness is Jesus Christ. I love the story in the Bible of when the Pharisees were about to stone a woman who committed adultery. Jesus said to them, "Let the one among you who is without sin be the first to throw a stone at her." The Pharisees walked away and the stoning did not occur. The woman was not condemned (John 8:1-11, New American Bible). I also believe Jesus showed His merciful heart when He was crucified next to two criminals. One man mocked Jesus, whereas the other man admitted his guilt and said that Jesus did not commit a crime. Jesus then said to him, "Amen, I say to you, today you will be with me in Paradise" (Luke 23:39-43). I think these instructions are a coded prescription for the healing of a person who has been harmed by another.

My father once shared with me the idea that holding onto un-forgiveness is like holding yourself in a prison of your own making. You call out for the wretched warden and find that the warden is you. You peer inside at the wretched inmate and discover that the inmate is you. I agree with my dad because that is how I felt. This is why forgiveness, to me, means glorious freedom. I don't say that it is easy – remembering in the case of sexual assault is not an option because the event is forever part of who we are, but choosing to forgive is a way of definitively taking back ourselves. And haven't we suffered enough? Haven't we paid for the thing we never chose enough?

I believe that truly good things, like emotional freedom, spiritual wholeness, and the courage to trust will come to us with a bit of effort, a bit of struggle, and a bit of broken-heartedness. I believe we grow to appreciate the good things in life a little every day and all the more for this good struggle; we change, we recover. So I highly recommend it. I believe forgiveness is epiphany, catharsis, release, and salvation for the one who extends the hand and to the one who receives it. Perhaps, at the end of the day, this wonderful work of reconciliation is what truly sets us free.

Chapter 22

B.L.E.S.S.

———

"But no matter how much evil I see, I think it's important for everyone to understand that there is much more light than darkness."

March Twenty-Eighth

"But try praying again,"
We offered on the night everything changed.
For example, "Dear God", we might say, "won't you please help us?"

To practice breath-taking in a whole new world
of her public shame,
To find good things in the goodness
of never-before-held fears.

To spite despair and the scream sounds
of our waking dreams.
To just keep singing, singing
till normal life noises can't condemn.

To scare away the phantom-feel of his hair
on her face, her neck, her arms, her person –
and the black bruises that
deepen in dark there.

To fist off flashbacks,
every sneaking, creeping sense of his weight on things,
and broken pinky swears of silence on violence in that house.

To nibble pizza, play card tricks,
or read the "Justice" chapter in bite-sized bits.
Or yes, my "survivor" story,
and no, I know nothing in life makes sense.

To hold at bay stunning lies she still believes,
ten years not counting
about her worth
her purpose
her due to loves that left her helpless.

To maintain hope and faith
in this hell-like place of voices
always wanting,
waiting,
measuring sanity against that of hospital room mates
who stay to stare and then leave.

"Dear God", we do pray,
"Hide her safe in your sweet arms,
each hour every day.
Send her angels and guard her heart,
though we doubt,
we fear you will not show up for us on this
and hopes like these.

But…Jesus…would you please?"
So we try them anyway on a Holy Thursday.
Thinking oh how He loves, oh how He must…
and then we see you,
our Light in the sky,
descend with hope and healing.
True safety now,
and a peace that we can claim on this,
the second night
that everything changed.

-Jenee

Jenee wrote the poem at the beginning of this book after visiting her friend in the hospital who was beaten, choked, burned, and raped. This last poem was written two weeks later. The vicious beatings and rape her friend endured occurred at the end of the writing of this book. No matter how many educational workshops I facilitate, health events I table, people I talk to, or books I write, rape still exists. It still happens. It happens more than we even know. And it will continue to. I am repeating myself, but I believe this is worth repeating: It happens to people of every gender, age, ethnicity, religion, socio-economic status or sexual orientation. It is an evil crime that too many people unfortunately experience. It is a sick and twisted reality our world continues to face. I pose this question to all of us: What will we do about it?

As hard as it is to hear of such horrific crimes and see the effects of them, I am so blessed to be able to do what I do. I sometimes don't even understand how lucky I am. I am continually inspired by the strength and courage of rape survivors and those who care about the issues of sexual violence. I've learned so much over the years by just being present in different communities, meeting people, and listening to them. The blessings I've received by doing this work are impossible to describe even though I see some of the worst things possible. But no matter how much evil I see,

I think it's important for everyone to understand that there is much more light than darkness.

Volunteering at THP has truly been a journey, and it has not been easy or always enjoyable. I have had many ups and downs over the years. But no matter how many horrible things I have heard or bad experiences I have had, I wouldn't change a thing. I do not regret anything and I wouldn't change these experiences for anything in the world. For me, volunteering at THP has been fun, educational, inspirational, challenging, difficult, and at times emotionally draining. Doing this work has affected me in positive and negative ways, but the good has far outweighed the bad. Ultimately, THP has allowed me to teach and impact the lives of many people. THP has helped me to understand some of my own skills, and helped me to be a better counselor and public speaker.

In six short years, I have become a more empathetic and sensitive person. I have attempted to understand things that I will never be able to fully understand and learned to try to put myself in someone else's shoes much more than I did before. I have become more educated on the prevalence of sexual violence, the very real effects it may have on people who experience it, and the options they may pursue if they want to. My listening skills have been enhanced, and I have learned to shut up and just listen when someone needs to talk. This has been an invaluable lesson to me as well as the people with whom I have interacted.

I do not believe it was easy for THP to take a chance on a man like me with no experience, but I am thankful and blessed that they did. I will always be grateful to Joan and the rest of THP for giving me an opportunity and allowing me to be a part of their family. Thank you to all of those who have taught me, inspired me, and shared your story with me. To my fellow volunteers: Thank you so much for voting me to become the "Volunteer of the Year" and for writing some of the kindest words about me. That was the best award I have ever won in my life, and I deeply cherish it.

Sexual violence is too complex and too big of an issue for me and the survivors you just met to tackle in one book. I cannot fully get into issues of laws, sentencing, policing, consent, perpetration, being a bystander, and other issues in one book. Each issue within sexual violence deserves its own book or books. The survivors you just met and I cannot cover all of the issues. We don't have all of the answers, but we believe this is something that hopefully connects with people and helps in some kind of way. There are so many issues, disagreements, and questions that cannot be contained in one book. Given that, I just want to leave you with ten things that I think are very important to understand:

1) Survivors are not to blame. If you are to blame anyone, blame a person who chooses to rape.

2) Do not think only women and girls are raped and sexually assaulted. Men and boys are also raped and sexually assaulted.

3) If someone discloses to you, please believe and listen to him or her.

4) Do not blame a survivor because of the clothes he or she wears. The clothes someone wears are completely irrelevant in every single rape that occurs.

5) Do not blame a survivor when alcohol or drugs are involved; there are plenty of people who rape sober and who are raped sober.

6) Do not blame survivors for being raped when they hang out with "that person". Many rapists are viewed as nice people.

7) Do not force survivors to do anything. They do not have to go to a hospital. They do not have to go to the police. They do not have to go to court. They can if they choose to. If they are looking for help, please provide them with resources and options, and be the bridge to those resources and options. Let them make the choice for themselves, but try to be that bridge.

8) Rape jokes hurt people. They can trigger survivors in re-experiencing horrific trauma.

9) Support survivors in what they need at the time.

10) Always understand that people can and do heal from sexual violence and other forms of violence as well. No matter how bleak things may seem, people can grow, get better, and heal in whatever way healing happens for them.

I firmly believe that sexual violence exists within every village, town, city, state, and country. It is disturbingly prevalent and damaging, and it can happen to anyone. Our responses to sexual violence need to be helpful and not hurtful. I have met many people who unfortunately do not know how to respond to incidences of sexual violence. It's not their fault; they just don't know. So I want to share with you one tool that may help if someone ever discloses that he or she has been raped or sexually assaulted. I ask that you "B.L.E.S.S." that person. Here is how:

B elieve: Believe that person if they disclose.

L isten: Listen to that person when they need to talk, cry, or scream.

E mpathy: Empathize with that person as best you can.

S afety: Ensure that person's physical, emotional, mental and spiritual safety.

S upport: Support that person in whatever they need at the time.

To the survivors out there, know that you are not to blame and you are not alone. If you have not been believed or fear you won't be believed, or if you feel like you are not supported or may not be supported at some point in the future, always understand that I and everyone you just met believe and support you.

Sexual violence is a difficult topic to think about and even harder to deal with. I understand that a wide range of emotions may have been ignited while reading this book, so I ask you to take care of yourself. Always remember to take care of yourself no matter what, and never stop doing the things you love that bring peace and joy to your life. Whether it is music, art, exercise, cooking, reading, sports, prayer, nature, or any of the other amazing gifts life has to offer: Embrace them. Do what you love to do, embrace all the beauty that exists within yourself and the world around you, and take care of yourself. And of course, reach out to someone if you need help. Talk to a family member or friend, find the right therapist, or seek out a religious or spiritual guide if needed. Life is very difficult to go through it alone, so please talk to someone you love and trust, and one who always has your best interest at heart.

I believe in hope and healing. I never would have written this book if I didn't. People do survive and grow from sexual violence, which I hope has been proven by all of the survivors in this book. However, sexual violence is not going away. Men, women, and children will continue to be raped and sexually assaulted. Our world suffers because of this.

Shira is a strong woman who has changed thousands of lives with her words, heart and soul. She is an amazing advocate who does everything in her power to help, teach, and raise awareness about the realities of sexual violence. She dedicates her life to it. However, I am saddened to write that Shira was raped during the final editing stages of this book by someone she loved.

I do not have all of the answers. I cannot give a clear, perfect one hundred percent reason as to why people rape. I have my opinions and theories, but they are only my opinions and theories. Sexual violence is extremely complicated and hard to deal with, but we can do more, and I believe we need to do more. I believe sexual violence is one of the worst crimes our world will continue to face. Will we take the issue of sexual violence more seriously or will we not? If we take the issue of sexual violence more seriously, how many ways will the world change for the better? If we don't take the issue of sexual violence more seriously, how many ways will the world change for the worse? The choice is ours. What will we choose?

ACKNOWLEDGEMENTS

———

~ First and foremost, I want to thank God and Jesus. I never would have done all that I have without you. I have no idea where I would be without you. You have saved my life multiple times. You have given me immense strength and hope in times of severe weakness and depression. I never even would have written a book if it weren't for you, nor could I have ever finished it without you. You have given me visions that I now understand the meanings of. I love you.

~ To my family, thank you for all of the love and support throughout my life. I know being related to a rape crisis counselor isn't the easiest thing. I am sorry if I have ever brought down a conversation or ruined a night because of the work I do, and I'm sorry if I have caused you any kind of suffering throughout this process. But this was something I had to do, and something I will continue to do. Always know that I am thankful to you for everything. You have all shown me different levels of compassion, faith, and hard work, which are so, so incredibly important. You have helped me throughout my life in a variety of different ways, which are too many to list right now. I wouldn't be who I am without you. I love you.

~ To my friends, thank you for the love and support. True friends are like family to me. As with my family, I'm sorry if I have caused you any kind of suffering throughout this process. But this was something I had to do, and something I will continue to do. I love you all. I cherish our talks, dinners, music and concerts. Keep listening to what moves and inspires you, and never stop. Follow what is in your heart.

~ To Joan, thank you for taking a chance on me. You gave me an opportunity that I will always be grateful for. You taught me so much by just one phone call. Thank you for everything.

~ To Aila, thank you for this interview that I believe will help more and more survivors who haven't seen their form of justice yet. I also believe it will help significant others have better responses to sexual violence. I will try my best to spread your words as far as possible. There really are too many people that need to hear from you.

~ To the THP staff and volunteers that I have worked with, thank you. Thank you for the lessons, good times, and life changes we were able to be a part of. Your hard work and dedication is extremely valuable in this world. Keep doing what you do. Your hard work does not go unnoticed.

~ To Alexis, you were the first one I told about this book. Thank you for supporting me and for contributing to this book. You always put a smile on my face. *Stay black and die*, and always keep rockin.

~ To Shira, you really are the most intense person I know. What we have accomplished together is truly amazing. I do not forget those moments, nor do I believe the people we helped forgot. You have suffered a lot, but you have a gift. No matter how hard life can be, always remember what you mean to the people you interact with and how much you have changed their lives.

~ To Megan, thank you for everything. You had the biggest smile out of anyone when I spoke about this book. I will never forget that smile. Your excitement, your stories, your writings, and your encouraging words inspired me in ways that are hard to describe. You were a huge part of this process. Thank you for having faith in what I was trying to accomplish. Never stop what you're doing, and please, write, write, and write some more.

~ To Jim, where do I begin? I never met a man like you. You were the first man I ever met who openly spoke about being sexually abused in a public forum. What you experienced is horrible, and the Catholic Church's responses to sexual abuse of children were and still are criminal.

Jesus challenged the religious leaders at the time, and I respect you more than you even know for doing the same thing during our time. I'm right there with you. Thank you for contributing to this book, supporting me in every single way, and introducing me to two other great men. You mean so much to a lot of people, especially men and boys who may never speak about being sexually abused.

~ To Don, thank you for being vulnerable and taking a chance. You did not know me, yet you came to my apartment to talk about sexual abuse. Our talk that morning was special. I am so thankful to have met you, and I know your words mean so much to others. You always wanted to just help one person. Well my friend, you have already helped more than one.

~ To Chris, as with Don, thank you for being vulnerable and taking a chance. You also did not know me, yet you came to my apartment to share your story. You are so incredibly intelligent, articulate, and insightful. Thank you for contributing to this book and for all the support you have given me. As with Jim and Don, your words will mean so much to people, but especially to men and boys. Any person who comes to you for help is lucky, because they found the right person to talk to.

~ To Corey, thank you for contributing to this book, our conversations about rape at 7am or midnight, and for the unconditional support. Our first engagement was truly interesting, especially given the weird exercises before the march began. I admire you so much for your passion of helping those impacted by sexual violence and raising awareness. You are one of the smartest people I know, and I am truly honored to help you with your own book. Never stop writing and speaking. You have so much to teach, and so many people need to learn. It's not their fault; they just haven't been taught yet.

~ To Timothy, thank you for all of the wisdom and times you have listened to me over the years. Your faith and prayers mean so much to me, and I know they help. You are a good man, and I'm thankful God connected us. I wish you all the best in everything you do.

~ To Mary, thank you for our friendship. Please keep writing and exploring. I promise that everything will be okay. Trust me, you will be fine and you will continue to grow.

~ To Rebecca, thank you for contributing at the end of this process. I saw how much you meant to those students. You have such wisdom for your age. Keep expanding on your passions within the criminal justice system and speaking out against sexual violence. I know you will be great at whatever you choose to do.

~ Last but not least, I want to thank Jenee, my co-facilitator, friend, editor, and spiritual guide. Words cannot truly describe how grateful I am to you for your words of encouragement, prayers, and edits. You edited a book about rape, which is not easy. All of the long hours, emails, phone calls, deep thinking, pain, and tears; you did it. This book would not be what it is without you. Words cannot fully describe how grateful I am. Thank you for everything.

REFERENCES

——

Lipkin, S. The Changeling's Lament. (2011). *Stone Telling*, 5. Retrieved from http://stonetelling.com/issue5-sep2011/lipkin-changeling.html

Lisak, David (2002). The Neurobiology of Trauma. Understanding Sexual Violence: The Judicial Response to Stranger and Nonstranger Rape and Sexual Assault Cases. The *National Judicial Education Program*. An unpublished article. Judicial education curriculum.

Made in the USA
Charleston, SC
04 September 2014